Expediting the Return to Work: Approaches in the Unemployment Compensation Program

Julie M. Whittaker
Specialist in Income Security

May 1, 2013

Congressional Research Service

7-5700

www.crs.gov

R43044

.

Summary

The most recent recession led to an unprecedented increase in the number of those unemployed for more than 26 weeks (the long-term unemployed). As a result, congressional interest in policy initiatives to expedite the return to work grew. This report examines a variety of initiatives and measures within the Unemployment Compensation (UC) program that might reduce long-term unemployment for beneficiaries.

Even before the recent recession began, large numbers of UC recipients exhausted their entitlement to regular state benefits before returning to work. In 2007, one in three recipients exhausted their benefits. In the depths of the recession, more than half of the recipients exhausted their regular benefits, with most of them continuing to receive unemployment insurance benefits through federally financed extended unemployment benefits. Based on current forecasts of a slow recovery and on trends that were apparent before the recession, it appears likely that the exhaustion rate will remain well above its pre-recession level for many years to come. The adverse consequences of not being able to find new work and of exhausting benefits can be severe for the recipients themselves, as well as for government budgets in terms of lost revenue and higher expenditures, and for the economy in lost output.

During and immediately following the recession, Congress provided incentives for states to adopt innovative ways of helping unemployed individuals return to work and enacted legislation that temporarily increased funding for various reemployment and training services. As the labor market continues to recover and the temporary funding ends, Congress may again consider policy initiatives that go beyond income replacement. These may include strategies that would speed up the reemployment of recipients who will not be returning to their previous employers.

After a brief description of the federal-state unemployment insurance system, this report examines trends in the duration of unemployment benefits and then reviews a wide range of approaches for speeding the return to work. The report emphasizes measures that have recently been considered by lawmakers or have been tried on an experimental basis, particularly if evaluations of their impacts on duration of UC benefit receipt are available.

Contents

Figures

Contacts

Introduction

Policy makers and analysts have searched for methods to speed the return to work of unemployment compensation (UC) recipients with varying levels of intensity. The most recent recession led to an unprecedented increase in the number of workers unemployed for more than 26 weeks (the long-term unemployed). As a result, congressional interest in policy initiatives to expedite the return to work grew. This report examines the current initiatives as well as previous demonstration projects within the UC system to reduce long-term unemployment and speed the return to work.

Overview of Unemployment Insurance Programs

Several unemployment insurance (UI) programs provide benefits to eligible workers when they lose their jobs. In most states, the regular UC program provides up to 26 weeks of income support through the payment of regular state benefits. The permanently authorized Extended Benefit (EB) program extends UC benefits if certain economic conditions exist within the state; that program is jointly funded by the federal and state governments. As in previous recessions, in June 2008, Congress created an additional temporary federally financed Emergency Unemployment Compensation (EUC08) program that further extended the maximum duration of benefit receipt; the authorization for this program ends on December 28, 2013 (December 29, 2013 in New York). In addition, several smaller state and federal programs provide benefits for other certain types of eligible unemployed workers. For detailed information on federal programs available to unemployed workers, see CRS Report RL34251, *Federal Programs Available to Unemployed Workers*.

Regular Unemployment Compensation

The cornerstone of an unemployed worker's income security is the joint federal-state UC program, which provides income support through the payment of UC benefits. The underlying framework of the UC system is contained in the Social Security Act (the Act). Title III of the Act authorizes grants to states for the administration of state UC laws, Title IX authorizes the various components of the federal Unemployment Trust Fund (UTF), and Title XII authorizes advances or loans to insolvent state programs. UC is financed by federal taxes under the Federal Unemployment Tax Act (FUTA) and by state payroll taxes under the State Unemployment Tax Acts (SUTA).

The UC program pays benefits to workers who become involuntarily unemployed for economic reasons and meet state-established eligibility rules. The UC program generally does not provide UC benefits to the self-employed, to those who are unable to work, or to those who do not have a recent earnings history. States usually disqualify claimants who lost their jobs because of inability to work, unavailability for work, who voluntarily quit without good cause, who were discharged for job-related misconduct, or who refused suitable work without good cause. To receive UC benefits, claimants must have enough recent earnings to meet their state's earnings requirements. Additionally, each state requires that the worker be able, available, and actively searching for work.

States determine weekly benefit amounts and durations. Maximum weekly benefit amounts in July 2012 ranged from $133 (Puerto Rico) to $653 (Massachusetts) and, in states that provide dependent's allowances, up to $979 (Massachusetts, with 13 dependents). In 2012, the average weekly benefit was just over $300. In most states, regular UC benefits are available for up to 26 weeks.[1] The average regular UC benefit duration in 2012 was just over 17 weeks. In the last week of January 2013, about 2.7 million unemployed workers were receiving regular UC benefits.

Extended Benefits and Temporary Programs

Extended Benefits

The EB program, established by the Federal-State Extended Unemployment Compensation Act of 1970 (P.L. 91-373), may extend UC benefits at the state level if certain economic conditions exist within the state. The EB program is permanently authorized, and is triggered when a state's insured unemployment rate (IUR) or total unemployment rate (TUR) reaches certain levels.[2] The federal government finances 50% of the EB program and states finance the other 50%.[3] Up to 34 states had active EB programs at some point during or after the 2007-2009 recession; by June 10 2012, 4 states had active EB programs.[4] As of the writing of this report, only Alaska had an active EB program.

Emergency Unemployment Compensation

On June 30, 2008, the EUC08 program was created by the Supplemental Appropriations Act of 2008 (P.L. 110-252). This was the eighth time Congress created a federal temporary program that extended unemployment compensation during an economic slowdown. State UC agencies administered the EUC08 benefit along with regular UC and EB benefits. Amended eleven times, at the program's peak four tiers of EUC08 benefits were available to unemployed workers in states with high unemployment rates; in states in which all four tiers of EUC08 benefits were available, eligible unemployed workers could receive up to 99 weeks of benefits combined from the regular UC, EB, and EUC08 programs. All tiers of EUC08 benefits will expire on the week ending on or before January 1, 2014.

---

[1] U.S. Department of Labor, Employment and Training Administration, *Significant Provisions of State Unemployment Insurance Laws Effective July 2012*, Washington, DC, September 2012, http://ows.doleta.gov/unemploy/content/ sigpros/2010-2019/July2012.pdf. For information on states offering fewer than 26 weeks of UC benefits, see CRS Report R41859, *Unemployment Insurance: Consequences of Changes in State Unemployment Compensation Laws*, by Katelin P. Isaacs.

[2] The IUR is the three-month average of the ratio of individuals receiving regular state UC benefits to all employed workers covered by the UC program. The TUR is the three month average of the ratio of unemployed workers (without regard to UC receipt) to all workers (employed and unemployed) in the labor force, based on the monthly Current Population Survey.

[3] Under the American Recovery and Reinvestment Act of 2009 (ARRA; P.L. 111-5), as amended, the federal government temporarily finances 100% of the EB program through the end of 2013.

[4] Idaho, Nevada, New Jersey, and Rhode Island. See http://ows.doleta.gov/unemploy/trigger/2012/trig_061012.html.

Long-Term Unemployment and Patterns of UC Benefit Exhaustion

Duration of Regular UC Benefits

From its inception, the UC program has been designed to provide temporary income support for eligible workers who lost their jobs, but has never been intended to last long enough to cover the entire spell of unemployment of every recipient. The Social Security Act of 1935, P.L. 74-271, left it up to each state to determine how long eligible unemployed workers would be allowed to receive benefits, as well as most other terms of the program. Initially, states set the maximum duration between 12 and 20 weeks, with 16 weeks being the most common.[5]

By the early 1960s, most states had increased the maximum duration to 26 weeks, where it remained until recently.[6] Each state sets its own rules to determine how long benefits can be collected. Nine states (Connecticut, Hawaii, Illinois, Louisiana, Maryland, New Hampshire, New York, Puerto Rico,[7] and West Virginia) provide uniform durations for all claimants who meet the qualifying-wage requirements. The rest have variable durations in which the state determines the limit on total benefits that a claimant can receive in a benefit year, generally based on the claimant's wages during a base period, and then divides that amount by the claimant's weekly benefit amount.

By 2013, 8 states that had provided UC benefits for up to 26 weeks acted to decrease their maximum UC benefit durations. Arkansas decreased its state UC maximum duration to 25 weeks, effective March 30, 2011. Florida decreased its maximum duration to a variable maximum duration, depending on the state unemployment rate and ranging from 12 weeks up to 23 weeks, effective January 1, 2012. Georgia decreased its maximum duration to a variable maximum duration that ranges between 14 weeks and 20 weeks, effective May 2, 2012. Illinois decreased its maximum duration to 25 weeks, effective January 1, 2012. Michigan decreased its maximum duration to 20 weeks, effective for individuals filing an initial claim for UC benefits on or after January 15, 2012. Missouri decreased its maximum duration to 20 weeks, effective April 13, 2011. North Carolina decreased the maximum UC duration from 26 weeks to a variable maximum duration, depending on the state unemployment rate and ranging from 12 weeks up to 20 weeks, effective July 1, 2013. South Carolina also decreased its maximum duration to 20 weeks, effective June 14, 2011.

Decisions by state and federal lawmakers about how long to provide unemployment benefits to eligible workers reflect difficult tradeoffs among several program goals and constraints. The main goals of the program have been to provide temporary income support to workers who lose their

---

[5] Saul J. Blaustein, *Unemployment Insurance in the United States: The First Half Century* (Kalamazoo, MI: W.E. Upjohn Institute for Employment Research), 1993.

[6] Two states provide longer durations: unemployed workers in Massachusetts may be eligible for up to 30 weeks of benefits and those in Montana may be eligible for up to 28 weeks of benefits. See U.S. Department of Labor, *Comparison of State Unemployment Insurance Laws 2012*, available at http://workforcesecurity.doleta.gov/unemploy/comparison2012.asp and CRS Report R41859, *Unemployment Insurance: Consequences of Changes in State Unemployment Compensation Laws*, by Katelin P. Isaacs.

[7] In federal UC law, the District of Columbia, Puerto Rico, and the Virgin Islands are considered states.

jobs and to help stabilize the overall level of economic activity by providing weekly cash benefits to eligible unemployed workers. But as the potential duration of benefits increases, the costs of the program also rise.

Moreover, the availability of UC benefits may lengthen the time that a recipient remains unemployed for at least two reasons. First, some individuals may not have as strong an incentive to quickly return to work while they are receiving UC benefits; the partial replacement of lost earnings enables them to enjoy more leisure. Second, many unemployed workers are liquidity constrained—that is, they do not have access to assets, loans, or other income to help maintain their consumption while they are looking for work. By providing temporary income support, the UC benefits enable those job-seekers to take the time to find a better job than they might have found otherwise.[8] For a more nuanced discussion and summary of the estimated effects of UC on the economy, labor market, and individual behavior, see CRS Report R41676, *The Effect of Unemployment Insurance on the Economy and the Labor Market*, by Thomas L. Hungerford.

There is no consensus on the magnitude of the impact of lengthening the potential duration of UC benefits on the length of time workers are unemployed. For example, some researchers suggest that a 13-week extension of available benefits would increase the average number of weeks of regular UC benefit receipt by one week[9] while others suggest up to a 2.5 week increase.[10] The magnitude of estimated impact may change by factors such as the general state of the labor market and the economy.[11] If the economy is weak, the impact of additional weeks of benefits on unemployment duration is likely to be smaller since the likelihood of finding is new job is smaller. In a strong economy where job opportunities are more plentiful, the impact on duration may be larger since the likelihood of reemployment is larger. Most of the studies examining the effects of the program have limited the focus to unemployed workers receiving benefits or workers who would be potentially eligible to receive benefits if they were to become unemployed. In addition, the effects of the program could spill over and affect the large number of unemployed workers who are not eligible for benefits (for example, new entrants and reentrants into the labor force). The chances of these UC-ineligible job-seekers finding a job may increase as some UC recipients reduce their effort searching for work.[12]

Trends in the Exhaustion Rate and in the Average Duration of Receipt

Two measures, the exhaustion rate and the average duration of receipt, are commonly used to characterize the length of time that UC recipients collect benefits. Both provide valuable information about how well the program is performing.

---

[8] Evidence for that effect is presented by Raj Chetty, "Moral Hazard vs. Liquidity and Optimal Unemployment Insurance," *Journal of Political Economy*, vol. 116, no. 2 (2008), pp. 173-234.

[9] David Card and Phillip B. Levine, "Extended Benefits and the Duration of UI Spells: Evidence from the New Jersey Extended Benefit Program," *Journal of Public Economics*, vol. 78 (2000), pp. 107-138.

[10] Lawrence F. Katz and Bruce D. Meyer, "The Impact of the Potential Duration of Unemployment Benefits on the Duration of Unemployment," *Journal of Public Economics*, vol. 41, no. 1 (February 1990), pp. 45-72.

[11] See for example Stepan Jurajda and Frederick J. Tannery, "Unemployment Durations and Extended Unemployment Benefits in Local Labor Markets," *Industrial and Labor Relations Review*, vol. 56, no. 2 (January 2003), pp. 324-348.

[12] One study estimated that a 10% increase in the UC benefit leads to about a one week reduction in the unemployment spell of an uninsured unemployed worker. See Phillip B. Levine, "Spillover Effects Between the Insured and Uninsured Unemployed," *Industrial and Labor Relations Review*, vol. 47, no. 1 (October 1993), pp. 73-86.

Exhaustion Rate

The exhaustion rate is an estimate of the percentage of recipients that use up or "exhaust" their entitlement to regular benefits. This is calculated by the U.S. Department of Labor (DOL) by dividing the number of average monthly final payments by the average monthly first payments. To allow for the normal flow of claimants through the program, the denominator lags the numerator by six months. For example, the exhaustion rate for the 12-month period ending in December 2012 is computed by dividing the average monthly exhaustions for the 12 months ending in December 2012 by the average monthly first payments for the 12-month period ending in June 2012.[13]

The exhaustion rate is important as an indicator of the adequacy of the regular state UC program in providing income support for unemployed workers while they are seeking new employment. By this measure, there has been a secular decline in the adequacy of the program that was apparent well before the start of the 2007-2009 recession (see **Figure 1**). During periods of low unemployment in the 1970s, about one in four UC recipients exhausted their entitlement to regular benefits (depicted by the solid line). By the late 1990s, the exhaustion rate had risen to one in three, even though the nation's unemployment rate was somewhat lower. In 2006 and 2007, with an unemployment rate of 4.6%, over 35% of UC recipients exhausted their entitlement to regular benefits. Over the three decades leading up to the recent recession, the exhaustion rate had risen by between three and four percentage points per decade.

---

[13] The exhaustion rate is based on the number of claimants drawing the final payment of their original entitlement for regular benefits. Although the maximum potential benefit was 26 weeks in most states until recently, many recipients in states with variable durations are not eligible for that maximum. As discussed in the next section, recipients with relatively short potential benefit durations are more likely to exhaust than are other recipients. Because most states offer up to 26 weeks of regular benefits, a person who exhausts regular benefits is generally considered to be long-term unemployed (even though the actual number weeks for which the person was unemployed may have been fewer than 26 weeks).

Figure I. Percentage of Recipients Exhausting Regular Unemployment Compensation Benefits, 1973 to 2012

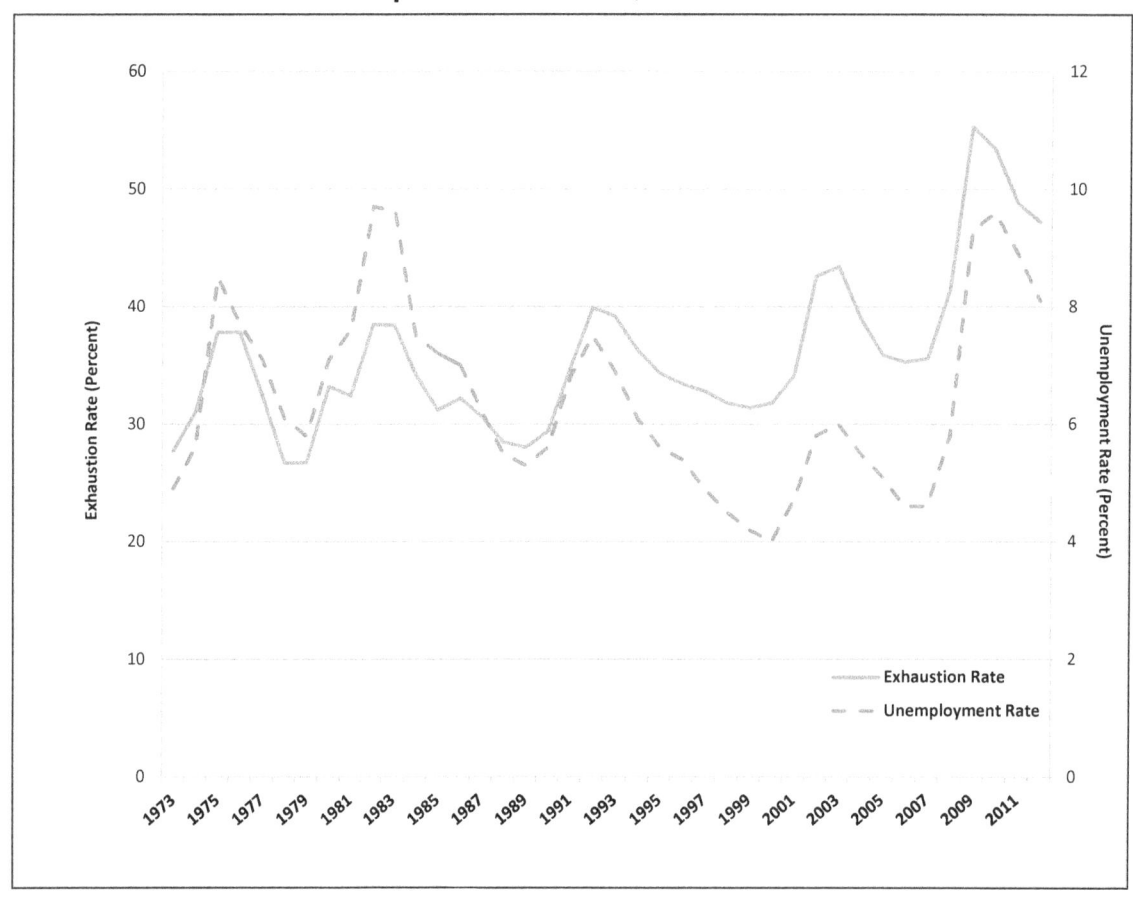

Source: CRS figure constructed by using data from the Employment and Training Administration and the Bureau of Labor Statistics, U.S. Department of Labor.

Average Duration of Regular UC Benefits

The average duration of receipt of regular UC benefits is the second measure used to characterize the length of time that recipients collect benefits. This is calculated by the DOL as the total number of weeks compensated for the year divided by the number of first payments. The average duration of receipt of benefits is an important component of the cost of the program. All else equal, the longer recipients collect benefits, the higher the cost. As with the exhaustion rate, a secular trend in the average duration was apparent before the recent recession (see **Figure 2**). In the early 1970s, the average duration was about 13 weeks, compared with about 15 weeks immediately before the recent recession.

Figure 2. Average Duration of Regular Unemployment Compensation, 1973 to 2012

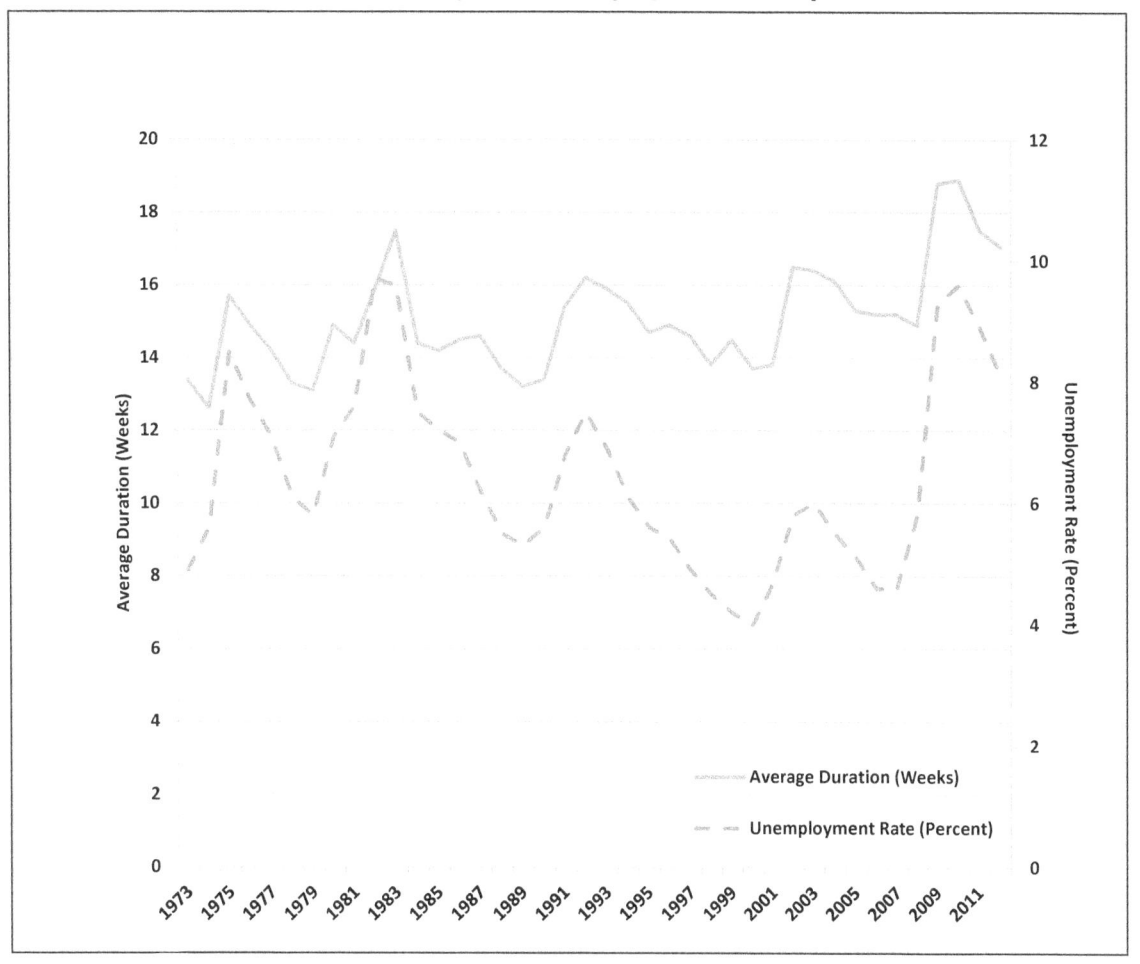

Source: CRS figure constructed by using data from the Employment and Training Administration and the Bureau of Labor Statistics, U.S. Department of Labor

As was the case in previous recessions, the downturn in the economy led to sharp increases in both measures. In 2009 and 2010, over half of UC recipients exhausted their entitlement to regular benefits and the average duration had risen to 19 weeks. Since then, as the labor market began to recover, the exhaustion rate and the average duration have begun to decline. The availability of EUC08 and EB benefits for unemployed workers who exhausted their regular benefits mitigated the adverse economic impact on recipients and on the economies of their communities, but probably added to the number of people counted as unemployed. As the recipients used that income to make purchases, the suppliers of those goods and services would have benefited as well, thereby stimulating demand in their communities. At their peak (in early 2010), the EUC08 and EB programs were providing benefits to about 6 million individuals.[14]

Early estimates of the possible impact of the increased availability of benefits on the measured unemployment rate range from an increase of 0.3 percentage points to approximately 1.0 percentage points.[15]

---

[14] Data are from the U.S. Department of Labor, available at http://www.workforcesecurity.doleta.gov/unemploy.

[15] These studies are summarized by Stephen A. Wandner, *The Response of the U.S. Public Workforce System to High* (continued...)

Explaining the Trends in Increased Exhaustion Rates and Average Duration of Benefit Receipt

The sharp increases in the exhaustion rate and in the average duration of receipt of regular UC benefits between 2007 and 2009 are not surprising in light of the severe weakening of the job market in that period. But cyclical variation cannot account for the long-term trends in the increased exhaustion rate and in the increased average duration that was apparent before that recession began.

Changes in Underlying UC Program

It is unclear if changes in the UC program itself are responsible. The regular UC program became less generous between 1973 and 2007, thereby reducing the incentive of recipients to remain unemployed: the average weekly benefit fell from 36% of average weekly earnings to 34%.[16] Nonwage compensation such as health insurance became more costly, implying that UC benefits replaced an even smaller percentage of total compensation. Benefits became subject to income taxation in 1979. And, the average potential duration of regular state benefits remained at about 24 weeks throughout the entire period.

Balancing the decreased relative generosity of the UC benefit, there has been some broadening of UC coverage of certain types of unemployed workers who would have not otherwise have been eligible for UC. The 2009 stimulus package, P.L. 111-5, provided incentive monies for states to "modernize" their programs to include a worker's more recent work history and two of four optional provisions relating to (1) part-time job-seekers, (2) voluntary separations for "compelling family reasons," (3) participation in qualifying training programs, or (4) dependents' allowances. The intent of these provisions was to broaden eligibility to cover more types of unemployed workers. Thirty-eight states plus the District of Columbia, Puerto Rico, and the Virgin Islands qualified for modernization incentive payments based on their use of more recent work history; most of those jurisdictions also qualified for additional incentive payments based on having one or more of the other optional provisions in their UC laws.

In addition, most older workers who lose their jobs no longer have UC benefits offset by Social Security benefits. As late as 2002, 20 states, the District of Columbia, Puerto Rico and the Virgin Islands offset the UC benefit by at least 50% of social security payments.[17] By 2012, only 4 states and the Virgin Islands offset at least a 50% of social security payments.[18] As a result, older workers who claim UC may have had a higher non-wage income and thus be able to extend duration of unemployment.

(...continued)

Unemployment during the Great Recession, Urban Institute Working Paper 4, September 2012, pp. 12-13.

[16] U.S. Department of Labor, Employment and Training Administration, *Employment and Training Financial Data Handbook 394*, Taxable and Reimburseable Claims Data, http://ows.doleta.gov/unemploy/hb394.asp.

[17] U.S. Department of Labor, Employment and Training Administration, *Comparisons of State Unemployment Laws 2002*, Chapter 5: Nonmonetary Eligibility, 2002, pp. 5-39-5-40, http://ows.doleta.gov/unemploy/pdf/uilawcompar/2002/nonmonetary.pdf.

[18] U.S. Department of Labor, Employment and Training Administration, *Comparisons of State Unemployment Laws 2012*, Chapter 5: Nonmonentary Eligibility, 2012, p. 5-45, http://ows.doleta.gov/unemploy/pdf/uilawcompar/2012/nonmonetary.pdf.

An additional change in the UC program that may have increased durations is the movement away from in-person filing for benefits in favor of filing by telephone or over the internet.[19]

Another reason for doubting that changes in the UC program itself are responsible for the increase in duration of UC receipt is that similar (or even steeper) increases in the duration of unemployment occurred for non-recipients. For example, between 1973 and 2007, the percentage of unemployed teenagers who were unemployed for more than six months more than doubled, even though very few of them would have been eligible for UC benefits. Likewise, substantial increases occurred among voluntary job leavers, reentrants into the labor force, and new entrants—individuals also unlikely to have qualified for benefits.[20]

In addition, the variance in potential durations of receiving UC insurance benefits has also had implications for the trends in the exhaustion rate. Research estimates find that states with higher average potential duration of benefits have a lower percentage of exhaustees—after controlling for unemployment levels.[21] Additionally, in a non-recessionary period of the late 1980s, researchers found that 26% of exhaustees had potential UC durations of less than 20 weeks as compared with only 12% of nonexhaustees having such low potential durations.[22] As states cut weeks of available benefits, the exhaustion rate is likely to increase in those states. In states that have broadened eligibility rules to allow some weeks of benefits to individuals who would have otherwise not have been eligible, those individuals may qualify for lower durations (and thus would be more likely to exhaust benefits).

Changes in the Labor Market

Researchers who have examined trends in the duration of overall unemployment—not necessarily focused on UC recipients—have developed several theories to explain the causes of increased durations of unemployment. However, no consensus has emerged.

Increase in Permanent Job Loss

On the demand side of the labor market, one development contributing to the increase in the duration of UC receipt has been the increased tendency for employers to permanently terminate workers, rather than to temporarily lay them off with the expectation that they would be recalled. Research by Burtless documented that increase and attributed it to changes in the industrial mix (especially the decline in manufacturing), as well as possible changes in employers' practices.[23]

---

[19] Christopher J. O'Leary, "State UI Job Search Rules and Reemployment Services," *Monthly Labor Review*, vol. 129, no. 6 (June 2006), pp. 27-37. Many observers believe this change depersonalized the process, making claimants feel less responsible for seeking reemployment, and thus lengthening UC spells.

[20] Bureau of Labor Statistics, U.S. Department of Labor, *Current Population Surveys 1972-2006*, Characteristics of the Unemployed: Table 31. Unemployed persons by age, sex, race, Hispanic or Latino ethnicity, marital status, and duration of unemployment, at http://www.bls.gov/cps/tables.htm.

[21] Stephen Woodbury and Murray Rubin, "The Duration of Benefits" in *Unemployment Insurance in the United States: Analysis of Policy Issues*, Christopher O'Leary and Stephen Wandner, eds. (Kalamazoo, MI: W.E. Upjohn Institute for Employment Research, 1997), pp. 211-283.

[22] Walter Corson and Mark Dynarski, *A Study of Unemployment Insurance Recipients and Exhaustees: Findings from a National Survey*, U.S. Department of Labor, Employment and Training Administration, Unemployment Compensation Occasional Paper 90-3, 1990.

[23] Gary Burtless, "Trends in the Structure of the Labor Market and Unemployment: Implications for U.S. (continued...)

The rise in permanent separations, rather than temporary layoffs, is important because workers who are no longer attached to an employer often take considerably longer to become reemployed. Even in 2011—with a total unemployment rate of almost 9%—only about 7% of unemployed workers on temporary layoff had been unemployed for more than six months; 52% of unemployed workers who had been permanently separated or who had completed temporary jobs had been unemployed that long.[24] Since most people who become eligible for UC benefits are workers who have either been permanently separated or been temporarily laid off, the shift toward permanent separations would directly lead to an increase in the duration of benefit receipt.[25]

Demographics and Aging Population

On the supply side of the labor market, the aging of the baby boom generation (individuals born between 1946 and 1964) likely contributed to increased durations and may continue to do so. In 1973, the oldest boomer was only 27. They are now mostly in their 50s and 60s. The Bureau of Labor Statistics (BLS) projects that individuals aged 55 and older will account for most of the net growth in the labor force between 2010 and 2020.[26]

Although older workers are less likely than younger workers to become unemployed, those who do so tend to have a more difficult time finding jobs. In 2011, for example, data from the Current Population Survey indicate that 55% of unemployed individuals aged 55 and older had been unemployed more than half a year, compared with 42% of younger unemployed persons.[27]

Studies suggest that older unemployed workers take longer to find new jobs, are less likely to find a job, and their new jobs replace a smaller fraction of previous earnings. Older workers are much more likely to be *dislocated* from their jobs. That is, they are more likely to have lost a job where they had long tenure and the separation from the employer is permanent.[28] Dislocated workers have a lower chance of finding new employment. In addition, those who do find employment typically earn substantially less than they did in their previous job.[29] For older workers, a job dislocation has more of an impact on earnings than for younger workers. A significant proportion of their previous high salaries may be attributed to job tenure; thus, wages from new jobs may be

(...continued)

Unemployment Insurance," Report submitted by IMPAQ International to the U.S. Department of Labor, 2008, available at http://www.impaqint.com/files/4-Content/1-6-publications/1-6-2-project-reports/Report%20-%202%20-%20Trends%20in%20the%20Structure%20of%20the%20Labor%20Market.pdf .

[24] Bureau of Labor Statistics, U.S. Department of Labor, *Current Population Surveys 2012*, Characteristics of the Unemployed: Table 29. Unemployed persons by reason for unemployment, sex, age, and duration of unemployment, http://www.bls.gov/cps/tables.htm.

[25] David Autor, *The Polarization of Job Opportunities in the U.S. Labor Market: Implications for Employment and Earnings*, Center for American Progress and Hamilton Project, 2010.

[26] Mitra Toosi, "Labor Force Projections to 2020: A More Slowly Growing Workforce," *Monthly Labor Review*, vol. 135, no. 1 (January 2012), pp. 43-64. During this decade, the number of individuals aged 55 and older in the labor force is projected to grow by 11.4 million; the number of labor force participants aged 25 to 54 is projected to grow by only 1.7 million; and 2.6 million fewer people under the age of 25 are projected to be in the labor force.

[27] Annual tables from BLS are available at http://www.bls.gov/cps/cpsaat31.pdf.

[28] Sewin Chan and Ann Huff Stevens, "Job Loss and Employment Patterns of Older Workers," *Journal of Labor Economics*, vol. 12, no. 2 (April 2001), pp. 484-521.

[29] For a summary of this research see Henry S. Farber, *Job Loss and the Decline in Job Security*, CEPS Working Paper no. 171, June 2008.

substantially lower. Likewise, facing lower levels of replaced earnings, older workers are also less likely to continue to work after job dislocation. Subsequently this increases their chances of early withdrawal from the labor market.

A Growing Mismatch

Finally, some of the increase in the duration of UC receipt could simply reflect a growing mismatch between the characteristics of job seekers and the characteristics that employers are seeking. This is often referred to as increased structural unemployment. For example, even though the educational attainment of the labor force has been rising, increasing returns to education suggest that the demand for more educated workers had been rising even more.[30] A growing gap between other types of harder-to-quantify skills supplied by job seekers and the skills demanded would also increase durations. For an in-depth summary of research examining changes in structural employment during the most recent recession, see CRS Report R41785, *The Increase in Unemployment Since 2007: Is It Cyclical or Structural?*, by Linda Levine.[31] Recent research suggests that the increase in structural unemployment may explain between 20% and 35% (or 1.0-1.75 percentage points) of the 5 percentage point increase in the unemployment rate between 2007 and 2010.[32]

Outlook Under Current Law

Assuming that over the next several years the nation's labor market continues to improve, it is likely that exhaustion rates will continue to fall from their recent record-setting levels, but long spells of unemployment will remain a serious problem for many UC recipients and therefore for the program itself. Full recovery in the labor market is expected to take many years. The Congressional Budget Office (CBO) projects that the annual unemployment rate will stay above 6% until 2017.[33]

In 2007—the last full year before the recent recession—the nation's unemployment rate stood at 4.6%. But, even with that relatively low unemployment rate, almost 36% of UC recipients exhausted their entitlement to regular benefits and the average duration of UC receipt was about 15 weeks.

In its latest projections, CBO forecasts that in FY2018, with a 5.5 % total unemployment rate, 8.0 million UC first payments will be made. On average, the recipients are forecast to receive $346

---

[30] *Economic Report of the President*, February 2010, pp. 221-222.

[31] Several economists have estimated how much structural unemployment increased and contributed to the steep rise of the unemployment rate from a pre-recession average of 4.6% in 2007 to 9.3% in 2009 and a still higher 9.6% in 2010. Most of the empirical studies whose results are summarized in the report relied to varying degrees on recent deviations from the negative relationship between vacancy and unemployment rates and from the positive relationship between the job-finding rate and the vacancy-unemployment ratio.

[32] See for example: Mary Daly, Bart Hobijn, and Rob Valletta, *The Recent Evolution of the Natural Rate of Unemployment*, Federal Reserve Bank of San Francisco (FRBSF), Working Paper no. 2011-05, January 2011; Marcello Estevao and Evridiki Tsounta, *Has the Great Recession Raised U.S. Structural Unemployment?*, International Monetary Fund, Working Paper no. 11/105, May 2011; and Nicoletta Batini, Oya Celasun, Thomas Dowling, et al., *United States: Selected Issues Paper*, IMF, Country Report No. 10/248, July 2010.

[33] Congressional Budget Office, *Baseline Economic Forecast—February 2013 Baseline Projections*, February 3, 2013, http://www.cbo.gov/publication/43902.

---

per week for 15.0 weeks, resulting in total outlays for regular benefits of more than $41 billion in that year.[34] Although CBO does not publish projections of UC exhaustions, simply extrapolating the trend depicted in **Figure 1** suggests that the exhaustion rate will remain at or above 40% through 2018.[35]

While it may not be possible to accurately predict how long it will take future UC recipients to find work, there is little, if any, basis for anticipating that the trends in the exhaustion rate and in the average duration of UC receipt that were apparent before the recession will be reversed. The aging of the labor force and the likelihood that new UC recipients will largely consist of workers who have been permanently severed from their employers, rather than temporarily laid off, will continue to make the rapid return to work difficult for many recipients. The reductions in the maximum duration of UC benefits recently enacted in eight states is likely to reduce the average duration of compensated unemployment in those states while increasing the percentage of their recipients who will exhaust their entitlement to benefits.[36]

Approaches for Expediting the Return to Work

How to quickly and efficiently get UC recipients back to work has long been a subject of interest for researchers and policy makers. The sharp increase in duration accompanying the recent recession has heightened interest. The American Recovery and Reinvestment Act of 2009 (ARRA; P.L. 111-5) and subsequent legislation provided temporary support for several activities. Congress continues to express interest in expediting the return to work and may consider additional measures.

This section examines a wide range of approaches that have been tried or proposed for shortening the duration of UC receipt and reducing exhaustions. For each approach, the potential benefits and limitations are discussed. The various approaches can be categorized by the primary mechanism by which, if successful, they would speed the return to work. First, the approach may help assure that UC recipients are pursuing effective job search methods and provide them with assistance in their search. Second, the approach may increase the payoff to recipients for quickly finding new jobs. Third, the approach may provide additional incentives to potential employers to

---

[34] CBO's unemployment compensation baseline as of February 2013 is available at http://cbo.gov/sites/default/files/cbofiles/attachments/43892 Unemployment%20Compensation.pdf.

[35] Equations developed by one of the authors of this report used data for 1973 through 2007 to estimate the relationship between the exhaustion rate and a linear time trend, the total unemployment rate, and the availability of a federal extension of benefits; a similar equation was used for the average duration of UC receipt. See Ralph E. Smith, *The Secular Rise in Unemployment Insurance and What Can Be Done about It*, Upjohn Institute, Working Paper no.11-177 (2011).

[36] In December 2012, those seven states accounted for only about one-fifth of the nation's UC first payments and a similar fraction of the national labor force and total unemployment. Calculations are based upon data from U.S. Department of Labor data (first UC payments) available at https://ows.doleta.gov/unemploy/5159report.asp and the BLS data (the national labor force and total unemployment) available at http://www.bls.gov/news.release/pdf/laus.pdf. In December 2012, the seven states accounted for 144,607 of the 804,359 first payments, 2.6 million of the 12.3 million seasonally adjusted unemployed, and 32.0 million of the 159.3 million seasonally adjusted civilian labor force. Since that time North Carolina has become the eighth state to enact legislation to reduce weekly benefits. The North Carolina reduction will not be in effect until July 2013.

---

hire and retain them. Fourth, the approach may improve recipients' employability by providing them with additional opportunities for education and retraining.[37]

Job Search Requirements and Assistance

Enforcement of job search requirements and the provision of various types of job search assistance have been shown to reduce the duration of UC receipt. Although all states have some type of requirements for the unemployed to be able, available, and actively seeking work, federal law did not require states to have such laws until recently. Under the Middle Class Tax Relief and Job Creation Act of 2012 (P.L. 112-96), states must require that "as a condition of eligibility for regular compensation for any week, a claimant must be able to work, available to work, and actively seeking work."

Historically, the enforcement of job search requirements and the provision of job search assistance went hand in hand because the Employment Service (ES) administered the work test and was prepared to assist UC recipients with their job search. The Wagner-Peyser Act of 1933 established the Employment Service as a system jointly operated by the U.S. DOL and state employment security agencies. The central mission of the ES is to facilitate the match between individuals seeking employment and employers seeking workers. Services are open to all without fees. Local ES offices offer an array of services to job seekers and employers, including career counseling, job search workshops, labor market information, job listings, applicant screening, and referral to job openings. States provide ES services through three tiers of service delivery: self-service, facilitated self-help, and staff-assisted. As the names of the tiers imply, progressively more active staff involvement is required as services range from Internet job postings to career counseling. Upon the establishment of the UC program in 1935, ES offices also began to administer the UC work test requirements. These offices monitor UC claimants to ensure that they are able to work, available for work, and actively seeking work. For the recently unemployed, the ES processes UC income support claims and helps the individual find new employment.

The relationship between the UC program and the ES, as well as the specific rules for enforcing the work test and providing job-search assistance, has varied over time and across states. For example, it used to be the general practice that UC recipients were required to periodically visit an ES office. But recipients are now much less connected to the ES than in the past and receive less assistance. A study by O'Leary and Eberts just before the recent recession estimated that "3 to 4 percent of ES registrants currently receive employment counseling, compared to 20 percent in the 1960s at the peak of ES funding." [38]

Substantial reductions in funding, as well as the expansion of transactions by telephone and computer, contributed to the decline. Federal support for the ES has not kept up with the growth in the labor force, except for a temporary increase during the recent recession.[39] Funding peaked

---

[37] Portions of this section are based in part on material presented in an earlier working paper by one of the authors of this report. See Ralph E. Smith, *The Secular Rise in Unemployment Insurance and What Can Be Done about It*, Upjohn Institute, Working Paper no.11-177 (2011).

[38] Christopher J. O'Leary and Randall W. Eberts, *The Wagner-Peyser Act and U.S. Employment Service: Seventy-Five Years of Matching Job Seekers and Employers*, report prepared for Center for Employment Security Education and Research, National Association of State Workforce Agencies, 2008, available at http://research.upjohn.org/reports/29.

[39] Stephen A. Wandner, *The Response of the U.S. Public Workforce System to High Unemployment during the Great* (continued...)

at about $840 million in 1995, falling to about $700 million in 2008. The decline in funding for the ES was temporarily reversed with the enactment of the ARRA in 2009, which supplemented regular funding with about $400 million in funds to be expended by the end of June 2011.

A survey of state agencies conducted by the National Association of State Workforce Agencies in 2003 found that in most states UC applications were made by telephone or computer and that the most common method of certifying that recipients had been actively seeking work was by automated telephone response.[40] A subsequent study estimated that only 13% of initial claims for benefits in 2006 were made in person; 15 years earlier, nearly all initial claims were made in person.[41]

The effectiveness of stronger enforcement of job search requirements and various methods of providing job-search assistance was demonstrated in a series of experiments conducted in the 1980s and 1990s where UC claimants were randomly assigned to treatment or control groups.[42] For example, in a widely cited experiment conducted for U.S. DOL in 1983 in Charleston, South Carolina, UC claimants in one of the treatment groups were notified that to continue receiving benefits they needed to report to the nearest ES office for placement-related services.[43] About one-quarter of them did not do so initially, although some of them subsequently complied. Some of the recipients voluntarily stopped collecting benefits rather than comply and others were denied further benefits. Consequently, on average the recipients in the treatment group received approximately one-half fewer weeks of benefits than did the control group, resulting in a savings to the UC program. Analysis of the timing of the impact indicates that it was largely the result of the reporting requirement, not any services provided.

Evaluations of experiments conducted in Tacoma, Washington (1986-1987) and in Maryland (1994) provided further evidence of the potential for reducing UC expenditures through a strengthened work test. Once again reductions in the duration of UC receipt were achieved largely through UC recipients opting not to report for required services, rather than from the services themselves.[44] A noteworthy feature of the Tacoma experiment was that it also tested the

(...continued)

Recession, Urban Institute, Working Paper no.4, September 2012.

[40] Christopher J. O'Leary, "State UI Job Search Rules and Reemployment Services," *Monthly Labor Review*, vol. 129, no. 6 (2006), pp. 27-37.

[41] Avraham Ebenstein and Kevin Stange, "Does Inconvenience Explain Low Take-Up? Evidence from Unemployment Insurance," *Journal of Policy Analysis and Management*, vol. 29, no. 1 (2010), pp. 111-136.

[42] Comprehensive descriptions of these and other reemployment-related evaluations are provided in Stephen A. Wandner, *Solving the Reemployment Puzzle: From Research to Policy* (Kalamazoo, MI: W.E. Upjohn Institute for Employment Research, 2010) and Christopher J. O'Leary and Randall W. Eberts, "The Wagner-Peyser Act and U.S. Employment Service: Seventy-Five Years of Matching Job Seekers and Employers," Report prepared for Center for Employment Security Education and Research (SESER), National Association of State Workforce Agencies (NASWA), 2008, available at http://research.upjohn.org/reports/29.

[43] Walter Corson, David Long, and Walter Nicholson , *Evaluation of the Charleston Claimant Placement and Work Test Demonstration* , U.S. Department of Labor, Employment and Training Administration, Unemployment Insurance Occasional Paper 85-2, 1985.

[44] Terry R. Johnson and Daniel H. Klepinger, *Evaluation of the Impacts of the Washington Alternative Work Search Experiment*, Unemployment Insurance Occasional Paper 91-4, 1991, and Daniel H. Klepinger, Terry R. Johnson, Jutta M. Joesch, and Jacob M. Benus, *Evaluation of the Maryland Unemployment Insurance Work Search Demonstration*, final report by Battelle Memorial Institute to the Maryland Department of Labor, 1997, available at http://wdr.doleta.gov/owsdrr/98-2/98-2.pdf.

impact of relaxing the work test; doing so substantially increased the average duration of UC receipt.

Several methods for improving the enforcement of job search requirements and providing job-search assistance have been enacted or proposed. Some involve strengthening the collaboration between the UC program and the ES. Others involve increased use of Reemployment and Eligibility Assessments, discussed below.

Worker Profiling and Reemployment Services

Since the beginning of the UC program in 1935, the ES has helped to enforce job-search requirements and provided UC recipients, as well as other job seekers, free job-search assistance. One approach that Congress may consider is to increase the size of grants going to states for ES activities or specifically for activities designed to reduce the duration of UC receipt. A targeted way of enforcing job search requirements and providing employment-related assistance to recipients begins with trying to determine which of the new UC claimants are at greatest risk of exhausting their entitlement to benefits. In 1993, Congress amended federal unemployment tax law and created the new requirement that each state maintain its own Worker Profiling and Reemployment Services (WPRS) program (P.L. 103-152). States must identify UC claimants who are likely to exhaust regular UC benefits. After identifying likely UC benefit exhaustees through statistical profiling models, states must use their WPRS systems to refer workers to reemployment services to the extent that these services may be provided with existing state and federal funding. At the time of the creation of the WPRS program, no new federal funding was made available to states to provide reemployment services to UC claimants. Existing funds allocated for Wagner-Peyser Act programs, including ES, may be used to provide these services to UC claimants.

A multi-state evaluation of the WPRS conducted soon after the program was implemented found that it appeared to be quite effective in reducing the duration of UC receipt, but not in increasing the employment and earnings of the recipients.[45] In five of the six states for which the researchers had reliable data, the average duration of UC receipt was reduced by between 0.2 and 1.0 week. Exhaustion rates were significantly reduced in three of the states. Moreover, the researchers found that the impacts on UC receipt were generally larger for the claimants who had relatively high profiling scores; that is, it appears that the profiling system was generally effective in its targeting mechanisms. About a year after the recipients were profiled, their estimated employment and earnings levels were essentially no different from those of the comparison group. The researchers found wide variation across states in the amount of services provided to recipients who were required to participate. In addition, they found that the states that had the largest estimated impacts on UC receipt tended to be the ones that provided the most services.

An analysis of Kentucky's program conducted by a different set of researchers estimated much larger effects.[46] In the previously mentioned multi-state evaluation, Kentucky's program was

---

[45] Their findings are summarized in Katherine P. Dickinson., Paul T. Decker, and Suzanne D. Kreutzer, "Evaluation of WPRS System," in *Targeting Employment Services*, Randall W. Eberts, Christopher J. O'Leary, and Stephen A. Wandner, eds. (Kalamazoo, Mi: W.E. Upjohn Institute for Employment Research, 2002), pp. 61-81.

[46] Dan A. Black, Jeffrey A. Smith, Mark C. Berger, and Brett J. Noel, "Is the Threat of Reemployment Services More Effective than the Services Themselves? Evidence from Random Assignment in the UI System," *American Economic Review*, vol. 93, no. 4 (2003), pp. 1313-1327.

---

estimated to reduce the average duration of unemployment by 0.2 weeks, whereas in the stand alone Kentucky analysis, the program was estimated to reduce the average duration in Kentucky by about 2 weeks. Moreover, from the timing of the recipients' withdrawal from the UC program, the researchers concluded that these large impacts were primarily due to the recipients opting to exit UC rather than comply with the participation requirements. The larger estimated impacts may well have been due to differences in sampling methods between the studies.[47] The observation that most of the estimated impacts appear to have resulted from the deterrent effect may be due to the quite modest amount of services provided in Kentucky; three-quarters of the participants who attended the mandatory orientation were referred to activities that typically lasted only four to six hours. Whether more intensive services would have had an impact beyond the initial deterrent effect is not known.

Budgetary constraints appear to have limited the extent to which profiled claimants receive services, especially activities that require substantial staff time. For example, among the almost 8 million individuals who received UC benefits in 2007, only 1.2 million were referred to services, even though twice as many subsequently exhausted their entitlement to benefits; of the 900,000 individuals who reported for services, only 400,000 were assessed and 100,000 were referred to education or training programs.[48]

For most of its history, few federal resources have been provided to specifically fund the WPRS program. Initially, no specific funding was provided for the program because it was assumed that it could be operated with existing funds for the ES and other sources.[49] In 2001 through 2005, Congress appropriated approximately $35 million per year for Reemployment Services Grants. No further federal funding for the WPRS program was appropriated thereafter.

Then, in 2009, $250 million was appropriated for Reemployment Service (RES) Grants as part of the stimulus funding provided by ARRA. These grants were made available to state agencies to spend in 2009 and 2010. Guidance from the Department of Labor to state workforce agencies indicated that the funds were to be used to provide job search and other employment-related assistance services to UC claimants, including counseling, testing, occupational and labor market information, assessment, and referral to employers.[50] State agencies were also encouraged to use these funds for upgrading their information technology; this includes updating the models they use to identify which claimants are most likely to exhaust their UC benefits before finding new jobs.

With a grant from the Department of Labor, the National Association of State Workforce Agencies (NASWA) is conducting a major study of the activities undertaken by the states with these RES grants, as well as other ARRA-funded workforce development and UC activities. Their examination of the early implementation of the provisions in states visited between December 2009 and June 2010 found that three-quarters of them indicated that the top priority use of the

---

[47]Black et al. constructed an experimental design based upon differences in services provided to profiled workers receiving the same score whereas the multi-state analysis used a random sample of persons profiled and created a treatment group from administrative data.

[48] Stephen A. Wandner, "Employment Programs for Recipients of Unemployment Insurance," *Monthly Labor Review*, vol. 131, no. 10 (2008), pp. 17-27.

[49] Stephen A. Wandner, *Solving the Reemployment Puzzle: From Research to Policy* (Kalamazoo, MI: W.E. Upjohn Institute for Employment Research, 2010), p. 92.

[50] U.S. Department of Labor, Employment and Training Administration, Training and Employment Guidance Letter No. 14-08, March 18, 2009, available at http://wdr.doleta.gov/directives/attach/TEGL/TEGL14-08.pdf.

RES funds was to expand services to claimants identified through their WPRS system.[51] Many of the states did not have an active RES program at the time that the funds from the ARRA became available. The majority of state administrators reported that funds were being used to increase the number or variety of job-search assistance workshops, provide assessment and career counseling services, or refer claimants to training. A major concern, however, was what would happen after the funds ran out. Many of the staff hired by the state agencies for the RES activities were temporary workers. It was not clear how many of them would be retained.

Reemployment and Eligibility Assessments

A related way of enforcing job search requirements and providing employment-related assistance to recipients is through Reemployment and Eligibility Assessments (REAs). Since 2005, the federal government has provided grants to state workforce agencies to fund REAs. These are in-person interviews with selected UC claimants to assure that they are complying with the eligibility rules, determine if reemployment services are needed for the claimant to secure future employment, refer the individual to reemployment services as necessary, and provide labor market information that addresses the claimant's specific needs. REAs replaced a previous Eligibility Review Program that had been funded by DOL in which UC claimants were interviewed to confirm their eligibility for benefits.[52]

In May 2012, DOL awarded $65.5 million in grants to 40 states, the District of Columbia, and Puerto Rico to implement or continue REAs "to help speed job seekers' return to work while maintaining integrity of UI system."[53] This was the eighth year that DOL awarded REA grants. The grants could be used to conduct in-person assessments, including the development of a re-employment plan and the provision of labor market information to the claimants, a complete review of their eligibility for UC benefits, and a referral to reemployment services.

The findings from a DOL-funded evaluation, conducted by IMPAQ International, of an REA experiment in Minnesota in 2005 suggest that REAs can save money and reduce the duration of compensated unemployment, although whether the magnitude of the impacts would be similar in other circumstances is not clear.[54] A noteworthy feature of the Minnesota experiment is that the participants and the control group were drawn from the UC claimants who ranked in the middle third of the profiled claimants in the study sites—that is, they were neither the ones who were considered most likely to exhaust (a group that was already being targeted) or those who were least likely to exhaust.

---

[51] Richard A. Hobbie and Burt S. Barnow, "Early Implementation of the American Recovery and Reinvestment Act: Workforce Development and Unemployment Insurance Provisions," report submitted by the Center for Employment Security Education and Research, National Association of State Workforce Agencies (NASWA) to the U.S. Department of Labor, January 2011, available at http://wdr.doleta.gov/research/FullText_Documents/ETAOP_2011-06.pdf.

[52] Stephen A. Wandner, *Solving the Reemployment Puzzle*, pp. 153-189.

[53] ETA News Release, May 7, 2012, available at http://www.dol.gov/opa/media/press/eta/ETA20120916.htm#.UJxo6Yaz624.

[54] Jacob Benus, Eileen Poe-Yamagata, Ying Wang, and Etan Bass, *Reemployment and Eligibility Assessment (REA) Study FY 2005 Initiative*, Final Report (IMPAQ International), 2008, available at http://wdr.doleta.gov/research/FullText_Documents/Reemployment%20and%20Eligibility%20Assessment%20(REA)%20Study%20Final%20Report%20March%202008.pdf.

The researchers found that UC claimants who were called in for multiple REA interviews received approximately one fewer week of benefits, had a lower rate of benefit exhaustion, as well as an increased likelihood of returning to work within six months of their initial UC claim with no significant effects on their wage rates or hours per week worked. Payments to ineligible claimants were reduced. These positive results, however, must be tempered by the failure to find significant impacts in North Dakota, which also participated in this REA initiative. Researchers suggest that this may have been the result of UC claimants in the control group receiving similar, though less intensive, services as were received by claimants in the treatment group or because of small sample size. (The impacts of the REA initiative in seven other states that had been selected to participate could not be assessed because of difficulties in those states acquiring data or constructing comparison groups.)

A subsequent evaluation of REA activities in Florida, Idaho, Illinois, and Nevada in late 2009 estimated reductions in UC exhaustions in three of the four states studied.[55] That evaluation, funded by the DOL and conducted by IMPAQ International, concluded that the savings from reductions in the number of weeks receiving UC and EUC08 benefits greatly exceeded the costs of the REAs in Florida, Idaho, and Nevada. No impact was found for the Illinois REA activities; researchers noted that the Illinois program was inconsistently implemented and was restricted to claimants with high-demand skills and that the sample size for the evaluation was small. The largest estimated savings were in Nevada, where REA claimants received about three fewer weeks of benefits than did claimants in a control group.

The DOL commissioned a follow-up study to determine why Nevada's REA program was more effective than the programs in the other states.[56] That study confirmed the substantial savings in UC benefits and found that the program was also effective in helping the claimants to obtain employment earlier than they would have in the absence of the program. The researchers suggest that Nevada's greater success with its program may have resulted from it being the only one of the state programs evaluated that provided both REAs and RES by the same staff. However, the design of the evaluation did not allow a direct test of that hypothesis.

The Middle Class Tax Relief and Job Creation Act of 2012 (P.L. 112-96) required that all individuals receiving EUC08 be "able, available, and actively seeking" work. An active work search for EUC08 claimants requires individuals (1) to register with reemployment services, as required by the state; (2) to actively search for work that is appropriate for the individual's skill level and labor market availability; (3) to maintain a record of work search activities; and (4) to provide work search activities records to the state when requested. In addition, P.L. 112-96 required states to provide reemployment and eligibility assessments to certain EUC08 claimants. EUC08 claimants must participate in reemployment services, if referred. P.L. 112-96, as amended, provides $85 in federal funding per EUC08 claimant who receives REAs.[57]

---

[55] Eileen Poe-Yamagata, Jacob Benus, Nicholas Bill, Hugh Carrington, Marios Michaelides, and Ted Shen, *Impact of the Reemployment and Eligibility Assessment (REA) Initiative*, IMPAQ International, 2011, available at http://wdr.doleta.gov/research/FullText_Documents/ETAOP_2012_08_Impact_of_the_REA_Initiative.pdf .

[56] Marios Michaelides, Eileen Poe-Yamagata, Jacob Benus, and Dharmendra Tirumalasetti, *Impact of the Reemployment and Eligibility Assessment (REA) Initiative in Nevada, 2012*, available at http://wdr.doleta.gov/research/FullText_Documents/ETAOP_2012_08_REA_Nevada_Follow_up_Report.pdf .

[57] These funds are affected by the Budget Control Act of 2011, P.L. 112-25. For details, see U.S. Department of Labor, Unemployment Insurance Program Letter, No. 13-13, March 8, 2013, http://wdr.doleta.gov/directives/attach/UIPL/UIPL_13_013_Acc.pdf.

Additional Incentives to Recipients

Another approach for speeding the return to work of UC recipients is to increase their payoff for taking a new job sooner. The underlying assumption behind this approach is that some recipients would search for work more intensively or would be more willing to accept job offers that they might otherwise have rejected if the rewards were larger. Two options that directly use this approach are reemployment bonuses and wage insurance. A third option—self-employment assistance—encourages UC recipients to take a new job sooner by helping them to develop a new business while they are still receiving benefits.

Reemployment Bonuses

The first option would provide a bonus to UC recipients for becoming employed in a new job within a given period of time. For example, the plan hypothetically could provide UC recipients with a bonus equal to four times their weekly UC benefits if they began a new job within 10 weeks of when they initially filed for benefits. If successful, such a plan could encourage some recipients to accelerate their job search and find a job sooner.

Legislative proposals that would encourage states to offer reemployment bonuses to eligible UC recipients were developed in the Clinton and George W. Bush Administrations, but were not enacted.[58] As part of President Clinton's proposed Reemployment Act of 1994 (introduced by request as H.R. 4040 in the 103rd Congress), states would have been permitted to use UC funds to provide bonuses to eligible claimants who found full-time employment with a new employer within 12 weeks from the date that they initially claimed UC benefits and retained employment for at least four months. States could offer bonuses that did not exceed four times the weekly benefit amount payable to the recipient under the regular UC program. Eligibility would have been limited to individuals who had been identified as likely to exhaust their entitlement to UC benefits through WRPS as described earlier.

As part of President George Bush's 2003 economic stimulus package, Personal Reemployment Accounts (PRAs) could be used by UC recipients for cash bonuses, as well as for purchasing a variety of employment-related services. The purpose of the PRAs was to provide persons likely to exhaust their UC benefits a choice in the type and source of reemployment services and to induce claimants and exhaustees to speed their reemployment by providing a bonus equal to the balance in their PRAs when they obtained new jobs. PRA recipients would have had to use funds within their accounts for some reemployment services that had been available free, such as training, if they chose to use those services.

These proposals were motivated, at least in part, by findings from experiments conducted in Illinois,[59] New Jersey,[60] Pennsylvania,[61] and Washington State[62] in the 1980s to evaluate the

---

[58] The discussion of the development of legislation in the Clinton and Bush Administrations draws heavily on Stephen A. Wandner, *Solving the Reemployment Puzzle: From Research to Policy* (2010), pp. 391-438.

[59] Stephen A. Woodbury and Robert G. Spiegelman, "Bonuses to Workers and Employers to Reduce Unemployment: Randomized Trials in Illinois," *American Economic Review*, vol. 77 (September 1987), pp. 513-530.

[60] U.S. Department of Labor, *The New Jersey Unemployment Insurance Reemployment Demonstration Project: Six-Year Follow-Up and Summary Report*, Unemployment Insurance Occasional Paper 96-2, 1996.

[61] U.S. Department of Labor, *The Pennsylvania Reemployment Bonus Experiment Final Report*, Unemployment Insurance Occasional Paper 92-1, 1992.

---

efficacy of variously designed reemployment bonus programs. The evaluations and subsequent reanalysis generally concluded that offering bonuses to UC recipients shortened their length of benefit receipt, especially when UC recipients also were offered job-search assistance and when the bonus programs were targeted to those UC recipients most likely to exhaust their benefits.[63] The size of the bonuses offered ranged from roughly three times the average weekly UC benefit amount to 10 times the weekly benefit. Depending on the experiment, recipients had between three weeks and thirteen weeks after being told they were eligible for a bonus to begin a new job.

Researchers found that such inducements did result in shorter durations of UC receipt, but not necessarily by enough to offset the cost of the bonuses. The largest estimated impact was in Illinois, which was the site of the first experiment. UC claimants who found a job within 11 weeks of filing for benefits and kept it for four months were eligible for a $500 bonus, which was about four times the average weekly benefit. Claimants offered this bonus had about a one-week shorter duration than claimants in the control group who were not offered the bonus. Estimated impacts in the other experiments were mostly around half that size.[64] One caution about the findings from the experiments is that a portion of the success of the bonus-takers could come at the expense of increasing the duration of unemployment of other job seekers (displacement effect) or of inducing more workers who lose their jobs to file for benefits in order to become eligible for the bonuses (entry effect).[65]

Analysis also suggested that targeting eligibility for bonuses toward UC claimants with an above-average likelihood of exhausting their benefits could add to their effectiveness.[66] Using statistical models like the ones used by state offices to profile UC claimants, researchers reanalyzed the results from the reemployment bonus experiments in Pennsylvania and Washington. In each case, the analysts found that restricting the bonus offers to half of the UC claimants—the ones estimated to be more likely to exhaust—would have increased the impact on UC durations. In the bonus design that provided a longer qualification period and a smaller bonus, the estimated savings in UC payments exceeded the cost of the bonuses.

The Clinton Administration's proposal (H.R. 4040, introduced in the 103rd Congress) closely followed the design of the Pennsylvania and Washington experiments, except that the proposal restricted eligibility to profiled UC recipients who were likely to exhaust their entitlement to benefits. That restriction was designed to reduce costs and to limit the extent to which the availability of bonuses might have induced some unemployed workers who expected to find new

---

(...continued)

[62] U.S. Department of Labor, *The Washington Reemployment Bonus Experiment Final Report*, Unemployment Insurance Occasional Paper 92-6, 1992.

[63] For additional information about the bonus experiments, see CRS Report RL31825, *Personal Reemployment Accounts: Results from Bonus Experiments*, by Linda Levine and Ann Lordeman, and Philip K. Robins, "Summary and Policy Implications," in *Reemployment Bonuses in the Unemployment Insurance System: Evidence from Three Field Experiments*, Philip K. Robins and Robert G. Spiegelman, eds., W.E. Upjohn Institute for Employment Research, 2001, pp. 249-274.

[64] Much of the difference between the estimated impacts in Illinois and the other sites was associated with the availability of up to 12 weeks of additional benefits through a federal extension that was available in Illinois during part of the enrollment period. The estimated reduction in the duration of UC receipt for the claimants who were eligible for the extension was about one and one-half weeks, whereas the estimated reduction for the claimants only eligible for regular UC benefits was about two-thirds of a week.

[65] Christopher J. O'Leary, Paul T. Decker, and Stephen A. Wandner, "Cost-Effectiveness of Targeted Reemployment Bonuses," *Journal of Human Resources*, vol. 40, no. 1 (2005), pp. 270-279.

[66] Ibid.

---

jobs quickly to file for benefits anyway in order to get the bonus. The Bush Administration's proposal, by combining potential bonuses with reemployment services into one account, differed sharply from the design of the original experiments. For example, most of the experiments linked the value of a bonus with the individual's UC benefit, while the size of the bonus that an individual could receive with the PRA would, instead, have been based on the balance remaining after paying for employment services.

Wage Insurance

Another way of providing an additional incentive to UC recipients to return to work more rapidly would be to offer them "wage insurance." Wage insurance subsidizes a fraction of the difference between the wage a worker earns in a new job and the wage earned in the old job for a limited period of time. Unlike reemployment bonuses, wage insurance would only provide payments to workers who incurred a wage loss. In that way, the subsidies would, in effect, compensate them for a portion of the financial loss they incurred when their old jobs were abolished.

As discussed above, many of the workers who lose their jobs, especially ones who have been with the same employer for many years, are unlikely to find new jobs that pay as much as the ones they lost. Even though UC provides workers with temporary income support while they search for new jobs, it does not compensate them for the possibly permanent reduction in their earnings that resulted from the job loss. Particularly for workers who lose jobs that they held for many years, the long-term reduction in earnings could greatly exceed the losses while unemployed. Wage insurance may help to induce those workers to accept lower-paying jobs that they might have been reluctant to take, as well as compensating them for a portion of their loss in earnings.

Opponents of wage insurance contend that such plans subsidize downward mobility, encouraging job seekers to accept lower-paying jobs rather than helping them to prepare for better ones.[67] Moreover, because it would only provide a benefit to workers who incur a reduction in their wages, workers who lose low-paying jobs are less likely to qualify.

Proposals for wage insurance, at least as an experiment, have been offered for many years, but have only been implemented on a very limited basis. P.L. 100-418, enacted in 1988, directed the DOL to conduct wage insurance demonstration projects for workers eligible for Trade Adjustment Assistance benefits, but the projects were never carried out because the agency was unable to secure sufficient state interest.[68]

Since 2002, wage insurance has been offered to certain workers aged 50 or older who are certified as eligible for Trade Adjustment Assistance (TAA) benefits.[69] If those workers accept a new job that pays less than the one they lost, the federal government will pay them half of the difference in wages for up to two years. Now called Reemployment Trade Adjustment Assistance (RTAA),

---

[67] For example, see Testimony of Jane McDonald-Pines, workforce issues specialist, Hearing Before the Senate Finance Committee on Trade and Globalization, June 6, 2007, available at http://www.finance.senate.gov/imo/media/doc/060607testjmp.pdf.

[68] Walter Corson and Joshua Haimson, "Wage Supplements for Dislocated Workers: the TAA Wage Supplementation Demonstration," report submitted to the U.S. Department of Labor, Employment and Training Administration by Mathematica Policy Research, Inc., 1995.

[69] For additional information about trade adjustment assistance for workers, see CRS Report R42012, *Trade Adjustment Assistance for Workers*, by Benjamin Collins.

the program provides eligible workers with a wage supplement that can total up to $10,000 over a two-year period. Earnings in the new job cannot exceed $50,000 a year. In 2011, $40 million was paid to more than 6,100 participants in the RTAA wage insurance program.

The President Obama's American Jobs Act (introduced by request as S. 1549 and H.R. 12 in the 112th Congress) would have established a "Reemployment NOW" program with $4 billion in direct appropriations to fund state-designed activities to assist the reemployment of eligible individuals. One of the allowable activities that states could undertake would have been to provide an income supplement to EUC08 claimants who secure reemployment at a lower wage than their separated employment. The benefit level would be determined by the states, although it could not be more than 50% of the difference between the worker's wage at the time of separation and the worker's reemployment wage. States would also establish a maximum benefit amount that an individual could collect. The duration of wage insurance payments would be limited to two years. Wage insurance under this proposal would also be limited to individuals who (1) are at least 50 years old; (2) earn not more than $50,000 per year from reemployment; (3) are employed on a full-time basis as defined by the state; and (4) are not employed by the employer from which the individual was separated.

Very little information is available to gauge the effectiveness of wage insurance in reducing the duration of unemployment or UC exhaustions. As with the reemployment bonuses, wage insurance could shorten the duration of unemployment by increasing the effective wage in the new job. If a fixed-length eligibility period begins while the job seeker is still receiving UC benefits, that feature could reduce UC outlays.

A version of wage insurance was tested in five cities in Canada in the mid-1990s. In that experiment, claimants who found a new lower-paying job within six months could receive an earnings supplement of 75% of their earnings loss (up to a cap) for up to two years. Evaluators found that the supplement appeared to have little impact on how quickly participants found new jobs. Its major effect was to partially compensate workers for the wage losses that they incurred.[70]

Self-Employment Assistance

Another way of providing an additional incentive to UC recipients to return to work more rapidly would be to make it easier for them to start their own businesses while still receiving benefits.

Self-employment is one potential pathway to exit a spell of unemployment. The regular UC program requires unemployed workers to be actively seeking work and to be available for work as a condition of eligibility for UC benefits. These requirements constitute a barrier to self-employment for unemployed workers who need income support.

The Self-Employment Assistance (SEA) program, created in 1993(P.L. 103-182) and made permanent in 1998 (P.L. 105-306), helps unemployed individuals establish their own businesses by providing them with temporary income support (in lieu of receiving regular UC) and access to entrepreneurial training and services.[71] SEA waives state UC work search requirements for those

---

[70] Howard S. Bloom, Saul Schwartz, Susanna Lui-Gurr, Suk Won Lee, Jason Peng, and Wendy Bancroft, "Testing a Financial Incentive to Promote Re-employment among Displaced Workers: the Canadian Earnings Supplement Project (ES), *Journal of Policy Analysis and Management*, vol. 20, no. 3 (2001), pp. 505-523.

[71] For a full discussion of the SEA program, its development, and its assessment, see CRS Report R41253, *The Self-* (continued...)

individuals who are working full time to establish their own businesses. SEA provides a weekly allowance in the same amount and for the same duration as regular UC benefits. It is available only to individuals who would otherwise be entitled to UC benefits and have been determined likely to exhaust their regular benefits. Most recently, provisions in the Middle Class Tax Relief and Job Creation Act of 2012 (P.L. 112-96) gave states the authority to expand SEA participation to certain claimants in the EB and EUC08 programs. Unlike reemployment bonuses and wage insurance, self-employment assistance is not primarily designed to reduce the duration of participants' current spell of compensated unemployment; but, if successful, the participants could become reemployed sooner and be less likely to need UC benefits in the future.

The current SEA program built on lessons learned from two self-employment demonstration projects conducted in the early 1990s in Massachusetts and Washington. Findings from these pilots were generally positive. In particular, the demonstration evaluation determined that the structure of the Massachusetts program, which became the model for the future SEA program authorization, was a cost-effective approach to promoting reemployment among workers.[72] The researchers concluded that participation in the Massachusetts SEA program significantly reduced participants' receipt of benefits and increased their total earnings over the 2½-year period after selection into the program.

Participation in the program by states as well as unemployed workers is limited. Currently, only Delaware, Maine, New Jersey, New York, and Oregon have active SEA programs for UC claimants, and in one of these states—New York—authorization for the program is scheduled to expire December 2013.[73] Total participation in the SEA program has ranged between 1,000 and 2,000 individuals per year since 2003.

In part, the small-scale nature of the program is likely due to the authorizing legislation requirement that SEA be budget neutral; that is, a state program may not incur additional costs above what the state would have spent on its regular UC program. The entrepreneurial training that SEA participants are expected to receive must come from other funding sources. Moreover, the number of individuals participating in the program may not exceed 5% of individuals receiving regular UC benefits in a state.

State officials report several challenges in operating their SEA programs. For example, the administrator of the UC program in Oregon (which operates one of the largest SEA programs) lists the reliance on a profiling system for identifying eligible participants that might not reflect their ability to start and manage a business as one challenge. Lack of funds for entrepreneurial training, limited capacity, and difficulty in monitoring long-term effectiveness are other barriers.[74]

(...continued)

Employment Assistance (SEA) Program, by Katelin P. Isaacs; Stephen A. Wandner, Solving the Reemployment Puzzle, pp. 289-340; and Stephen A. Wandner, *The Response of the U.S. Public Workforce System to High Unemployment during the Great Recession*, Urban Institute, Working Paper no. 4, September 2012, pp. 41-44.

[72] U.S. Department of Labor, Employment and Training Administration, 1995, *Self-Employment Programs: A New Reemployment Strategy, Final Report on the UI Self-Employment Demonstration*, Unemployment Insurance Occasional Paper 95-4, by Jacob M. Benus, Terry R. Johnson, Michelle Wood, Neelima Grover, and Theodore Shen, available at http://wdr.doleta.gov/research/FullText_Documents/op_04-95.pdf.

[73] Louisiana and Maryland also have SEA programs authorized, but they are not active. See U.S. Department of Labor, Comparison of State Unemployment Insurance Laws, 2012, available at http://workforcesecurity.doleta.gov/unemploy/comparison2012.asp.

[74] David Gerstenfeld, "Self Employment Assistance in Oregon," presentation to NASWA National UI Directors' (continued...)

There are many options that might be considered if Congress were to expand the program, such as having the federal government, rather than the states, pay the SEA benefits or providing stronger incentives for the states to use a portion of their funds from the Workforce Investment Act for entrepreneurial training.[75] Even with such actions, though, it is unlikely that self-employment would be an attractive alternative for a large fraction of UC recipients.

Additional Incentives to Employers

Another approach for speeding the return to work of UC recipients is to increase the payoff to potential employers to hire them. Banning discrimination on the basis of employment status and providing subsidies to employers are two methods that have been considered in recent years. A related option is to provide an incentive to employers to retain workers who otherwise would have been laid off; short-time compensation, discussed below, uses this approach.

Prohibition of Discrimination

Employers may favor job applicants who are currently working over applicants who are unemployed, particular job seekers who have been unemployed for many months. Employers may, at least informally, rank job applicants by their duration of unemployment and hire from the front of the queue because they consider lengthy unemployment to be a signal of poor worker quality (that is, low productivity). In effect, long-term unemployment can stigmatize workers. Employers may also be reluctant to hire the long-term unemployed because they believe the group's skills have atrophied during their lengthy time away from the workplace.

The American Jobs Act as proposed by President Obama in 2011 (introduced by request as S. 1549 and H.R. 12 in the 112th Congress) would have established the Fair Employment Opportunity Act of 2011, prohibiting employment discrimination against the unemployed. Designed to eliminate the economic burdens imposed by discrimination against the unemployed, the act would prohibit discrimination in job advertising and hiring practices. The act appears to be modeled on Title VII of the Civil Rights Act of 1964, which prohibits discrimination in employment on the basis of race, color, national origin, sex, or religion.

The Fair Employment Opportunity Act would prohibit employers and employment agencies from discriminating on the basis of employment status. Most public and private employers would be covered, although private employers who have fewer than 15 employees would be exempt. Covered employers and employment agencies would be prohibited from publishing an advertisement or announcement stating that individuals who are unemployed are not qualified for the employment opportunity or that such individuals would not be considered or hired. Other prohibited acts include the failure or refusal to consider or to hire an individual because of that individual's status as unemployed.

(...continued)

Conference, October 22-25, 2012, available at http://naswa.org/assets/utilities/serve.cfm?gid=8a9fc78d-dbf9-4513-95f8-f8cea733628a.

[75] For these and other recommendations for encouraging more states to adopt and use the SEA program, see Stephen A. Wandner, *Solving the Reemployment Puzzle*, pp. 336-337.

Enforcing such legislation could be challenging. Identification of discriminatory advertising should be straightforward, but more subtle forms of discrimination may be more difficult to prove. Compared with the victims of post-hiring types of discrimination, it is often harder for rejected job-seekers to establish why they were less favored. They generally have less information on which to base a discrimination complaint than do individuals who are already employed. Nonetheless, patterns of hiring discrimination could be identified, for example, through testing in which pairs of individuals with similar backgrounds, except for their current employment status, apply for the same job opening.[76] Moreover, recent research on the effectiveness of age discrimination legislation in facilitating the reemployment of older workers suggests that such legislation can make a difference.[77]

Tax Credits

Another method of encouraging employers to hire unemployed workers is to provide them with a subsidy for doing so, thereby reducing their cost. The subsidies could be to public employers, private employers, or both. In recent years, the main legislative focus has been on the use of the tax system to offer incentives to private employers. Tax credits have often been the vehicle for providing eligible employers subsidies either to expand total employment or to encourage employment of members of certain groups of workers such as disadvantaged individuals. But with the exceptions of the now-expired credits provided in the Hiring Incentives to Restore Employment Act (HIRE) of 2010 (P.L. 111-147) and in the unemployed veterans parts of the Work Opportunity Tax Credit (WOTC; P.L. 112-56), tax credits have not been specifically designed to promote the employment of unemployed individuals. Congress may consider options for renewing the expired targeted tax credits or creating new ones.

Under the provisions of HIRE, employers who hired certain previously unemployed workers after February 3, 2010, and before January 1, 2011, could be exempted from their share of the Social Security taxes paid on behalf of those workers. In addition, if they retained the workers for at least one year, the employers would be eligible for up to a $1,000 tax credit. Although the legislation was characterized as providing an incentive to hire individuals who had been unemployed for at least two months, it did not actually require them to have been actively seeking work during that period. To qualify, employees needed to certify that they had not been employed for more than 40 hours during the 60-day period on the date they started employment. It was not necessary that they had been previously employed before the 60-day period. Thus, new entrants to the labor force, as well as individuals who had been actively seeking work, could qualify.

The WOTC is a non-refundable tax credit for employers who hire individuals of certain targeted groups.[78] It replaced the Targeted Jobs Tax Credit (first authorized in 1978 by P.L. 95-600) in 1996. Through the end of 2011, for-profit employers were entitled to a credit against their federal income tax liabilities for hiring members of eligible groups, including members of families receiving benefits under the Temporary Assistance to Needy Families (TANF) program and other

---

[76] Marc Bendick, Jr. and Ana P. Nunes, "Developing the Research Basis for Controlling Bias in Hiring," *Journal of Social Issues*, vol. 68, no. 2 (2012), pp. 238-262.

[77] David Neumark and Joanne Song, *Barriers to Later Retirement: Increases in the Full Retirement Age, Age Discrimination, and the Physical Challenges of Work*, University of Michigan Retirement Research Center, Working Paper WP2012-265, September 2012, available at http://www.mrrc.isr.umich.edu/publications/papers/pdf/wp265.pdf.

[78] For additional information about the WOTC, see CRS Report RL30089, *The Work Opportunity Tax Credit (WOTC)*, by Christine Scott.

groups thought to experience employment problems regardless of general economic conditions. The credit was calculated as 40% of the first-year wages paid to the qualifying individual, up to a maximum amount of wages. For most qualified individuals, the maximum amount of first-year wages for calculating the WOTC was $6,000. ARRA extended the WOTC to cover unemployed veterans who had been discharged or released from active duty in the Armed Forces within five years of their hiring date and had received UC for not less than four weeks during the one-year period ending on the hiring date.

The VOW to Hire Heroes Act of 2011 (P.L. 112-56) expanded the targeted group for qualified unemployed veterans and made the WOTC refundable for certain non-profit employers. Employers hiring a veterans certified as having aggregate periods of unemployment of at least four weeks but less than six months in the year prior to being unemployed and employing them for at least 120 hours could claim a credit of 25% of $6,000 of first-year wages; if employing them for at least 400 hours, a credit of 40% of $6,000 of first-year wages could be claimed. Larger credits could be claimed for hiring veterans who had been unemployed at least six months. The act allowed employers to claim the WOTC for individuals certified as qualified veterans who began work before January 1, 2014.

Several bills introduced in the 112th Congress also would have offered employers tax credits to induce them to hire unemployed workers, especially individuals experiencing longer-term unemployment. President Obama's American Jobs Act of 2011 (S. 1549 and H.R. 12) would have added as a targeted group for purposes of the WOTC individuals who had been unemployed for at least six months during the one-year period prior to being hired. For those long-term unemployed who are hired and remain on a firm's payroll at least 400 hours, an employer would be able to claim a non-refundable income tax credit of 40% of the first $10,000 in wages paid during the worker's first year of employment. They would be eligible for a smaller credit if the worker remained employed for 120 hours to 399 hours. Under certain circumstances, tax-exempt employers could take the credit. Other bills introduced in the 112th Congress included H.R. 2120, which would have expanded the definition of a WOTC targeted group to include individuals who had exhausted entitlement to EUC08, and H.R. 1663, which would have provided a temporary tax credit for certain small businesses that hired unemployed individuals who had received unemployment benefits and resided in a county with an unemployment rate that exceeded 4%.

The use of targeted subsidies as a means of increasing the employment opportunities for members of specific groups has had mixed reviews.[79] Analyses of the Targeted Jobs Tax Credit found that the majority of jobs filled by employers who claimed the credit would have been filled without the credit. That is, they were not used to create new jobs. But for a targeted subsidy, the key issue is whether it succeeded in reshuffling the queue in favor of members of the targeted groups. On the one hand, because the cost of employing those individuals is reduced by the subsidy, they become more attractive to potential employers who are familiar with the program. On the other hand, some evidence was found of a stigmatizing effect, whereby some employers may have viewed the government's offer of a subsidy as evidence that there was something wrong with those job seekers.[80]

---

[79] For a summary of the literature, see CRS Report R41034, *Business Investment and Employment Tax Incentives to Stimulate the Economy*, by Thomas L. Hungerford and Jane G. Gravelle.

[80] Gary Burtless, "Are Targeted Wage Subsidies Harmful?," *Industrial and Labor Relations Review*, vol. 39, no. 1 (October 1985), pp. 105-114.

There is little basis to predict the impact of providing a tax credit to employers based on their hiring individuals who had been unemployed for a period or who were UC recipients (or were at risk of long-term unemployment or benefit exhaustion). An experiment in the 1980s in which employers who hired certain UC claimants and retained them for at least four months could receive a subsidy attracted few participants.[81] In addition to the issues concerning cost and windfalls associated with providing a tax credit for hiring individuals who would have been hired without the credit, lawmakers would need to consider potential spillover effects on members of the groups already targeted. The addition of this group could help the others by increasing the subsidy's visibility among potential employers and perhaps diminishing any stigma associated with it. But their inclusion could reduce employment opportunities for others to the extent that employers favor members of the newly eligible group.

GeorgiaWorks and Related State Programs

Various state-initiated short-term subsidy programs have also been used to encourage employers to hire unemployed workers. Georgia developed a program, GeorgiaWorks, to subsidize the wages of workers for a short period that received considerable attention. During the subsidy period, the newly hired workers would receive on-the-job experience and training. In addition, employers could determine whether they want to retain the new hires after the subsidy ended. That program was singled out by President Obama in his September 2011 address on his proposed jobs plan.[82]

The GeorgiaWorks program, begun in 2003, offers employers in that state an opportunity to train and assess UC recipients at no cost, while providing the recipients an opportunity to train with a potential employer. In its current structure, UC recipients can be voluntarily placed with an employer for a maximum of 24 hours per week for up to eight weeks. The Georgia agency pays the participant a training stipend and provides workers compensation coverage. The employer is under no obligation to hire the participant after the subsidy period ends.

From 2003 to 2009, the GeorgiaWorks program expanded rapidly, growing from about 400 participants in its first year to 3,000 participants in 2009. In September 2010, participation increased several fold with the expansion of eligibility to include unemployed workers who were not receiving UC benefits. But in 2011, with a change in the administration of the Georgia Department of Labor, the program was sharply reduced in size and scope. Eligibility was again restricted to UC recipients and the stipend was reduced from $600 to $240. The new labor commissioner said that spending had gotten out of control and that too few of the participants were trained and hired by the employers with whom they had been placed.[83]

---

[81] This was one of the treatments tested in a reemployment bonus experiment in Illinois. UC claimants who found a job within 11 weeks could provide their new employer with a document that the employer could forward to the state agency; if the employer retained them for four months, they could receive $500 from the agency. Only 3% of the claimants who participated in this part of the experiment were responsible for any bonus payments, compared with 14% of the claimants who participated in the part in which the claimants themselves received the same size bonus. See Stephen A. Woodbury and Robert G. Spiegelman, "Bonuses to Workers and Employers to Reduce Unemployment: Randomized Trials in Illinois," *American Economic Review*, vol. 77, no. 4 (1987), pp. 513-530.

[82] From the transcript of the Address by the President to a Joint Session of Congress, September 8, 2011: "This jobs plan builds on a program in Georgia that several Republican leaders have highlighted, where people who collect unemployment insurance participate in temporary work as a way to build their skills while they look for a permanent job."

[83] Mark Butler, state labor commissioner, from a segment on the PBS News Hour on October 12, 2011, "Georgia (continued...)

The potential benefits and limitations of short-term subsidy programs are illustrated by the data and debates about the merits of the GeorgiaWorks program. Data provided by the state's Department of Labor indicate that about 40% of the participants were placed in clerical occupations and that about 35% of the 7,500 participants who completed the program between 2003 and 2009 were hired by the employer with whom they had been placed. Opponents argue that the jobs in which the participants are often placed are the kinds of low-paying jobs temp agencies help firms fill without any training and point to the low percentage of the participants retained after the subsidy ends. Supporters contend that the program provides UC recipients with an opportunity to gain new skills and enhance their resume, even if they are not hired by the same employer.

Other states also launched short-term subsidy programs. For example, in 2010, Texas began its Texas Back-to-Work Initiative (TBTW). That program provides a subsidy of up to $2,000 to employers for hiring eligible first-time UC claimants previously earning less than $15 per hour. To qualify for the $2,000 TBTW subsidy, an employer is required to provide the claimant with at least 30 hours of work per week and is required to retain the claimant for at least 120 days. Smaller subsidies are available to employers for claimants who were retained for between 30 and 119 days. In April 2012, the executive director of the Texas Workforce Commission testified that more than 25,000 individuals had been placed in jobs through this program and that these placements had reduced the average duration of participants' unemployment receipt by nine weeks.[84]

Also in 2010, New Hampshire began its Return to Work Initiative. It is a voluntary program in which employers can take on eligible UC claimants for up to six weeks of structured supervised training of no more than 24 hours per week. The participants continue to receive UC benefits and must continue to search for work during non-training time unless otherwise exempted. Participants can remain in the program if they exhaust UC benefits prior to the end of the six-week period, but their UC benefits are discontinued. Claimants with a definite recall date within six weeks and those who do not register for employment services are not eligible.

In 2011, a workforce development board in Connecticut, The WorkPlace, launched a pilot program called Platform to Employment (P2E) to increase employment opportunities for long-term unemployed in southwestern Connecticut. Eligible individuals are offered a five-week preparatory program, including resume writing, interview preparation, self-marketing, and other skills. This is followed by placement with employers for an eight-week trial period. With support from several foundations, the program is scheduled to expand to 10 cities around the country in 2013, beginning with Chicago, Cincinnati, Dallas, and San Diego. Projects in the new sites will focus on long-term unemployed individuals over the age of 50 or who are military veterans.[85]

(...continued)

Works Jobs Training Program, a Peach or the Pits." It can be viewed at http://www.pbs.org/newshour/bb/business/july-dec11/georgiaworks_10-12.html.

[84] Testimony of Larry Temple, Executive Director, Texas Workforce Commission, before the House Ways and Means Committee, Subcommittee on Human Resources, "Moving from Unemployment Checks to Paychecks: Implementing Recent Reforms, April 25, 2012, available at http://waysandmeans.house.gov/uploadedfiles/larry_temple_testimony.pdf.

[85] Platform to Employment, "Successful Connecticut Program Putting the Long-Term Unemployed Back to Work Will Go National" at http://www.platformtoemployment.com.

In 2012, Utah began its Small Business Bridge Program, providing a subsidy to small businesses (up to 100 employees) that hire workers by June 30, 2013, and retain them for at least one year. Firms can receive a subsidy of between $3,000 and $4,000 per job created, with the amount based on the wages paid. In addition, a $500 bonus will be paid for each individual hired who was receiving UC at that time.

Also in 2012, Wisconsin initiated its Wisconsin Workers Win (W3) pilot program, modeled on the GeorgiaWorks program. UC recipients in their first 20 weeks of collecting benefits can be voluntarily placed with an employer for up to six weeks working 20 to 24 hours per week. The recipients continue to receive UC as well as an additional $75 weekly stipend. The employers must state their willingness to provide training and supervision. They are required to carry workers' compensation coverage, but not to pay wages or benefits, and are not obligated to retain the participants after the six-week period. Up to 500 UC recipients are expected to participate in the program during its first year.

The 112th Congress did incorporate some of these ideas into P.L. 112-96, which provides further encouragement to states to try out short-term wage subsidies to help UC recipients return to work. It allows up to 10 states to create and conduct demonstration projects to improve and accelerate the reemployment of UC claimants. These state reemployment demonstration projects could use UC funds to provide subsidies for employer-provided training, such as wage subsidies, or provide direct reimbursement to employers who hire individuals receiving UC to pay part of the cost of wages that exceed the individual's prior benefit level. The reimbursement may not exceed the weekly benefit amount of an individual. Subsidies for employer-provided training could include on-the-job training or other work-based training programs. The approved demonstration projects must last between one and three years, be completed by the end of 2015, and include an evaluation of its impact on participants' skill levels, earnings, and employment retention. As of the publication date of this report, no state demonstration project has been approved.[86]

Short-time Compensation

Short-time compensation (STC), sometimes called work sharing, is a program that provides pro-rated unemployment benefits to workers whose hours have been reduced in lieu of a layoff. STC may be helpful to a firm and its workers during an economic downturn or other periods when employers determine that a temporary reduction in work hours is necessary. In the states that operate STC plans, workers whose hours are reduced under a formal work sharing plan may be compensated with STC. Unlike the other options described in this report, the purpose of STC is to give employers an incentive to retain workers, thereby reducing the number of individuals who might otherwise become unemployed.[87] STC programs can provide macroeconomic benefits by preserving jobs during cyclical downturns and maintaining consumption. Participating employers can use it as a means of avoiding the costs associated with hiring and training new workers when business picks up; workers can benefit from reduced layoffs.

---

[86] See http://www.ows.doleta.gov/unemploy/jobcreact.asp for lists of state applications and U.S. DOL determinations.

[87] For a comprehensive description of STC, its usage, and legislative history, see CRS Report R40689, *Compensated Work Sharing Arrangements (Short-Time Compensation) as an Alternative to Layoffs*, by Julie M. Whittaker. Additionally see Stephen A. Wandner and David E. Balducchi, "Work Sharing," in Stephen A. Wandner, *Solving the Reemployment Puzzle: From Research to Policy*, 2010, pp. 341-390.

In a typical STC plan, a firm that must temporarily reduce the total number of hours worked by its 100-person workforce by 20% could accomplish this by reducing the work hours of its entire workforce by 20%—from five days to four days a week—in lieu of laying off 20 workers. Workers whose hours are reduced would receive 80% of their regular weekly earnings plus 20% of the UC benefit they would have been entitled to had they been laid off. As UC generally replaces almost half of an average worker's wages (up to a cap and with considerable variation among states), STC benefits would in this example amount to about 10% of the worker's full-time earnings. Employees would therefore receive a combined income of about 90% of their full-time wages as compensation for four days of work.

STC plans have never reached many workers in the United States, though they have been much more frequently used in several other developed countries. A recent study of the use of STC in the United States concluded that, "with the possible exception of Rhode Island, the overall scale of the STC program operating in the 17 states was too small to have substantially mitigated the aggregate job losses these states experienced in the recent recession. Expansion of the program within STC states as well as to states without the program is necessary for STC to be an effective counter-cyclical tool in the future."[88]

Many states have not enacted STC legislation and, within the states that have, few firms and workers have participated. At its peak usage during the recent recession, about 1.5% of UC recipients were STC participants.[89] Those STC participants accounted for less than 0.1% of the U.S. labor force. In comparison, over 5% of the labor force in Belgium, almost 2% of the German labor force, and over 1% of the labor force in several other European nations and Japan were in STC programs at around that time.[90] Some of the higher usage in other countries may reflect institutional and cultural differences; for example, higher fractions of workers in Belgium and Germany are represented by trade unions and there is more of a tradition of unions, management, and government jointly determining working arrangements. In addition, differences in who ultimately bears the cost of the plans may also be important, as discussed below.

An assessment of the impact of STC programs in 16 Organisation for Economic Co-operation and Development (OECD) countries during the recent recession concluded that they "played an important role in preventing many workers from unnecessarily facing unemployment during the 2008-09 crisis in a number of countries."[91] However, the authors noted that some of the support provided by these programs could have funded jobs that employers would have maintained without that support. They also cautioned that, as the economies in those countries emerge from the recession, the STC programs could impede economic restructuring.

Employers who are planning to lay off workers and are aware of the STC program may decide that it is not worthwhile for them to participate. For example, production technologies may make

---

[88] Katharine G. Abraham and Susan N. Houseman, *Short-Time Compensation as a Tool to Mitigate Job Loss? Evidence on the U.S. Experience during the Recent Recession*, Upjohn Institute, Working Paper no. 12-181, March 2012.

[89] In the first week in June 2009, about 140,000 individuals were participating in STC programs and 9.3 million individuals were receiving regular state UC, EB, or EUC08 payments. Weekly program data are provided by DOL on the spreadsheet, "Persons Claiming UI Benefits in Federal Programs (Expanded)," available at http://www.ows.doleta.gov/unemploy/finance.asp.

[90] Alexander Hijzen and Danielle Venn, *The Role of Short-Term Work Schemes During the 2008-09 Recession*, OECD Social, Employment and Migration Working Paper no. 115, January 2011, http://dx.doi.org/10.1787/5kgkd0bbwvxp-en.

[91] Hijzen and Venn, 2011, p. 38.

it expensive or impossible to shorten the work week. One obstacle that generally does not occur elsewhere is that the STC payments made to their employees may be treated like regular UC benefits for the purpose of determining a firm's unemployment tax rate. Because those tax rates are experience-rated, the employer may ultimately pay the full cost of the STC payments, just as it would if the workers had been laid off.[92] Likewise (and, again, unlike elsewhere) workers may be reticent because the STC payments are treated as regular UC benefits for the purpose of determining their remaining entitlement to benefits if they are subsequently laid off. Because firms facing slack demand might first reduce hours and then lay off workers, their employees might want to preserve their eligibility for the maximum number of weeks.

In addition, lack of awareness on the part of employers appears to have been a major barrier to participation among the states that have STC legislation. The director of the Rhode Island Department of Labor and Training, whose state has had one of the highest percentage of UC claimants participating in its STC program, attributes much of their relative success to their very active promotion of the program. In addition to dedicating several agency employees specifically to the program, they trained all of their UC claim-takers to monitor layoff patterns to identify employers that might benefit from using STC.[93]

Many states have either not opted to enact STC plans or, if they have such plans, have not aggressively marketed them. The administrative costs of STC programs have been a concern for state workforce agencies. In many states, STC is still paper-based and states approve employers' plans on a case-by-case basis. In addition, STC may increase processing costs for the state agency relative to layoffs because, for a given firm, work sharing affects a larger number of workers than if the firm were to lay off workers to achieve a comparable reduction in hours.

In an effort to expand the use of STC in lieu of layoffs, P.L. 112-96 included provisions intended to clarify the definition of STC and to provide incentives to states to adopt and modify STC programs. That legislation provides federal financing for 100% of STC benefits for up to three years in states whose program meets the definition of an STC program specified in the law. (A transition period is provided for states with existing STC programs that do not meet the new definition.)

Under the new legislation, employers would voluntarily submit written STC plans for approval by the relevant state agency. Eligible workers would receive UC on a prorated basis and would be able to participate in state-approved training. Employees would meet the availability for work and work search requirements while collecting STC by being available for their workweek as required by the state agency. Employers who provide health and retirement benefits would be required to certify that these benefits would continue to be provided under the same terms and conditions as though employees' workweeks had not been reduced or to the same extent as other employees not participating in the STC program. On August 13, 2012, U.S. DOL announced the availability of nearly $100 million in grants for states to implement or improve existing STC programs.[94]

---

[92] Experience rating may not result in the entire cost being passed on to the employer if, for example, the firm is already being charged the maximum rate or subsequently goes out of business. However, for employers who reimburse their state unemployment funds for benefit payments attributable to service in their employ, such as state and local governments, STC would not be a cost-effective option.

[93] Testimony of Charles J. Fogarty before the Senate Finance Committee on the Success of the Rhode Island WorkShare Short-Term Compensation Program, November 10, 2011, available at http://www.finance.senate.gov/imo/media/doc/Fogarty%20Testimony.pdf.

[94] U.S. Department of Labor, *Unemployment Insurance Program Letter*, No. 27-12, August 13, 2012, (continued...)

Retraining

Some workers who have lost their jobs may need to acquire new skills before they can return to work. Those displaced from jobs held for many years in an occupation or industry that is declining are especially at risk of exhausting their benefits before they have found new jobs. Their skills may have become obsolete and not readily transferable to other sectors. Long spells of unemployment resulting from structural changes could be used as opportunities to develop new skills. Training-related issues that the may be of congressional interest include the rules governing eligibility for receipt of UC while in training and the reauthorization and funding for retraining displaced workers through Title I of the Workforce Investment Act.

Retraining While Receiving Unemployment Compensation

Each state sets its own rules concerning the payment of UC benefits to individuals who are participating in a training program, subject to the federal requirement that a state cannot deny benefits to an individual for failure to be available for work during a week if the individual is in training with the approval of the state agency. But federal law does not specify the criteria that the states must use to approve training. In general, states limit approval to vocational or basic education training, thereby excluding regularly enrolled students from collecting UC benefits under this provision.

In 2009, Congress encouraged states to expand their support of training for UC recipients through the previously noted unemployment modernization incentive provisions in ARRA (the 2009 stimulus package; P.L. 111-5). One way states could qualify for an incentive payment was to amend their UC legislation to provide extended compensation to recipients in qualifying training programs. The provision could not be subject to discontinuation. To qualify, the state's UC legislation had to enable unemployed workers who had exhausted their entitlement to regular UC benefits to continue receiving benefits for at least 26 weeks if they were enrolled and making satisfactory progress in a state-approved training program or in a Workforce Investment Act training program that was preparing them for entry into a high-demand occupation. The final date for receiving incentive payments was September 2011. State legislators had to decide whether the one-time financial incentive was a sufficient inducement to make this change in their UC legislation. Ultimately, 15 states and the District of Columbia took up the option.[95] The effects of this provision have not yet been evaluated.

Lawmakers may want to consider whether to offer states additional incentives to provide retraining opportunities to UC recipients and whether to require states to modify their existing programs. For example, the Expanding Training Opportunities Act of 2012 (S. 2095) that was introduced would have expanded the types of training that may be considered approved training while an individual is receiving UC to specifically include any coursework necessary to attain a

---

(...continued)

http://wdr.doleta.gov/directives/corr_doc.cfm?DOCN=4749.

[95] To qualify for the maximum modernization payment, a state's UC law needed to include an approved alternative base period plus two of four optional provisions. These optional provisions related to the training extension, the treatment of part-time job-seekers, voluntary separations for compelling family reasons, and the payment of dependents' allowances. Of the 41 jurisdictions that had an approved alternative base period, 28 qualified with a part-time provision, 21 with a voluntary separations provision, 7 with dependents' allowances, and 16 with the training extension.

recognized postsecondary credential if that individual is likely to exhaust his or her regular UC, and the credential can be attained within a certain time. The proposal defined "recognized postsecondary credential" as a credential consisting of an industry-recognized certificate, a certificate of completion of an apprenticeship, or an associate or baccalaureate degree.

Workforce Investment Act[96]

For many years, the federal government has funded training and education programs that can help unemployed workers acquire new skills, thereby increasing their employment opportunities and earnings. These programs include training authorized by the Workforce Investment Act (WIA), as well as educational assistance through Pell grants and subsidized loans. Although training and education funded by these programs can reduce the likelihood that their participants will incur future spells of long-term unemployment, this is usually not their immediate purpose. Indeed, participation in a training or education program (at least on a full-time basis) likely will delay their reemployment. It is an investment intended to pay off by putting the participants on a higher-earning career trajectory than they otherwise would have.

WIA is currently the primary federal program that supports workforce development activities, including job search assistance, career development, and job training. WIA establishes the One-Stop delivery system as a way to co-locate and coordinate the activities of multiple employment programs for adults, youth, and various targeted subpopulations. The delivery of these services occurs primarily through more than 3,000 One-stop career centers nationwide. The authorization for appropriations for most programs under the WIA expired at the end of FY2003. Since that time, WIA programs have been funded through the annual appropriations process. About $1.2 billion was appropriated for dislocated worker activities under Title I of WIA for FY2012. Unemployed individuals are generally eligible for dislocated worker activities if they have been terminated, laid off, or notified that they will be terminated or laid off; sufficiently attached to the workforce, for example by being eligible for UC benefits; and are unlikely to return to their previous industry or occupation.

WIA implements a "work first" approach to workforce development, with placement in employment being the first goal of the services provided. Unemployed workers who participate in the WIA program generally receive at least "core" services, including the provision of workforce information. Some then receive more intensive assistance, such as the development of individual employment plans while others receive retraining support, generally in the form of vouchers that can be used to pay eligible education and training providers, such as community colleges and vocational schools.

Retraining (whether provided in a community college or elsewhere) is generally much more costly than the other employment-related services and involves much more of a commitment by the participants themselves. Generally, the offer of retraining support through WIA is only supposed to be made after the program staff determine that the core and intensive services are not

---

[96] A much more comprehensive discussion of the Workforce Investment Act is provided in CRS Report R41135, *The Workforce Investment Act and the One-Stop Delivery System*, by David H. Bradley. Recent WIA reauthorization proposals are described in P.L. 112-96 section of CRS Report R42658, *Workforce Investment Act (WIA) Reauthorization Proposals in the 112ᵗʰ Congress: Comparison of Major Features of Current Law and H.R. 4297*, by David H. Bradley and Benjamin Collins.

sufficient to enable a participant to obtain employment and that the participant has the background and ability to benefit.

Mixed results from two evaluations of WIA suggest that selective use of retraining can be effective but that care needs to be taken that the retraining is appropriate for the participant's interests and ability and likely to lead to reemployment. An evaluation of the WIA program by Heinrich and others was based on administrative data collected for about 60,000 displaced workers in 12 states who entered various WIA activities between mid-2003 and mid-2005.[97] About 20,000 of those participants received retraining assistance. The rest only received counseling and related job search services. Administrative data were used to track the employment and earnings of these participants for up to four years after they entered the program.

Researchers estimated that the participants in their sample increased their earnings by being in WIA, but with considerable variation across states and types of services provided. Particularly relevant is their conclusion that their study shows "little evidence that training produces substantial benefits."[98] Eighteen months after most of the participants had ended their training, their employment and earnings were not much higher than those of the WIA program participants who had only received non-training services. The researchers emphasized, however, that methodological issues make it difficult to be as confident in the estimates as one would like.

An earlier evaluation by Hollenbeck and others estimated the impacts of WIA activities on participants in seven states who left the program between mid-2000 and mid-2002 using similar methodology, but found larger impacts. Administrative data were used to track the employment and earnings of about 90,000 participants in WIA displaced worker activities and a comparison group through the end of 2003. Researchers estimated significant gains for the displaced workers who participated in any WIA activities. The estimated gains for the displaced workers in WIA training activities (about 50,000 of the participants) were also significant and persisted for at least two years after leaving the program. But these gains were smaller than those of the displaced workers who had only received non-training services.[99] As with the more recent evaluation, caution should be used in interpreting these estimates because it is possible that subtle differences between the groups being compared could affect the results.

---

[97] Carolyn J. Heinrich, Peter R. Mueser, Kenneth R. Troske, Kyung-Seong Jeon, and Daver C. Kahvecioglu, New Estimates of Public Employment and Training Program Net Impacts: A Nonexperimental Evaluation of the Workforce Investment Act Program, LaFollette School Working Paper no. 2009-013 (University of Wisconsin-Madison), 2009. The final report to the Department of Labor on which that paper is based is available at http://wdr.doleta.gov/research/ FullText_Documents/Workforce%20Investment%20Act%20Non- Experimental%20Net%20Impact%20Evaluation%20-%20Final%20Report.pdf.

[98] Heinrich et al., 2009, p.55.

[99] Kevin Hollenbeck, Daniel Schoeder, Christopher T. King, and Wei-Jang Huang, *Net Impact Estimates for Services Provided Through the Workforce Investment Act*, Employment and Training Administration, U.S. Department of Labor, 2005, http:.//wdr.doleta.gov/research/FullText_Documents/Net%20Impact%20Estimates%20for%20Services%20Provided% 20through%20the%20Workforce%20Investment%20Act-%20Final%20Report.pdf.

Acknowledgement

Ralph E. Smith, Consultant in Economics, wrote this report. Readers with questions about the UC program and expediting the return to work may contact Julie M. Whittaker.

Author Contact Information

Julie M. Whittaker

Specialist in Income Security
jwhittaker@crs.loc.gov, 7-2587

www.ingramcontent.com/pod-product-compliance
Lightning Source LLC
Chambersburg PA
CBHW080632290526
45790CB00007B/3038